Embracing Your Higher Self

A Practical Guide to Enlightenment

Dr. Zach

Dedication

This work is dedicated to Doris Berk, my hard-working and idealistic mother, who taught me that our work is not over until the downtrodden are uplifted and that, if any among us are suffering, then we all are suffering.

Copyright

A Note to Readers

Welcome! I'm happy you are curious enough about the topic of embracing your Higher Self or have a desire to become enlightened that you opened up this book to look inside. If you continue delving deeper into this work, I promise that you won't be disappointed. I consider myself an enlightened individual, which straight out isn't a supernatural achievement. It's one of the greatest human achievements but not as impossible as many people believe it to be. I promise you that enlightenment is attainable without having to join a monastery or committing to becoming a monk. That is why I created a meditation app entitled the *HappCo Meditation Journey* ("HMJ") and wrote this book, *Embracing Your Higher Self*. My definition of enlightenment is simply the ability to embrace your Higher Self for most of the day. The HMJ is a proven path that is available to you without you ever having to leave home. The beauty of technology allows you to take it anywhere.

My Beliefs and Your Experiences

In this book, I want to state upfront that I present ideas and writings of some of the greatest spiritual teachers, and I reference them. I also present my beliefs and speculations. The Buddha advised his students that they must trust their inner voices and be primarily guided by them. He also said not to rely solely on the "authorities" but to put it all together and make your own decisions on what truth is and what is right for you. The quest for truth is quite a challenge. Your experiences and conscious awareness are your final judge of things. I'm only trying to assist you in your journey.

I wrote this book for four reasons. To provide: (1) An in-depth and innovative exploration on the subject of enlightenment; (2) an opportunity for you to become informed and educated about an effective pathway to enlightenment; (3) a way for you, who might be interested in downloading the HMJ app, to first assess if its underlying ideas and strategies make sense to you; and (4) the business community with an understanding on how valuable and impactful a mindful, enlightened workforce can have on the quality of a corporate environment. Chapter 16 is devoted solely to the workplace. Regardless of these four reasons, I had no interest in writing a book, whetting your appetite about enlightenment, and then not giving you an opportunity to embrace your Higher Self.

Whether you are a serious meditator, a dabbler in meditation, or one who has never meditated before and now wants to get serious about it, you will find this book valuable. Wherever you are in your spiritual journey, if you want to embrace your Higher Self, help yourself to be transformed, and help the planet, you have come to the right place. I believe that achieving enlightenment is probably the most significant objective you can strive for, not only to increase your level of happiness and well-being but also to help all of humanity and the planet. I challenge you to join me in this endeavor.

I did not write this book to present a purely cognitive treatise on enlightenment, even though you will find valuable and insightful information here. It's my sole objective to help you embrace your Higher Self. That is why I wrote this book and created and produced the guided meditation program (HMJ) to get you there.

I planned for some time to write a book about my personal experiences and the HMJ program. While I was in a five-year stretch producing the HMJ program (which is now available on the App Store and Google Play, I discovered we learn better when we are in the alpha state (a brain state associated with meditation). It was then I decided to write brief informative talks and insert them into each meditation session. Then it dawned upon me I had enough material compiled from my talks for a book. [1] So, this book is composed mainly of talks, stories, and mini lectures that I give in the HMJ. Since the HMJ audio is 90% guided meditations and 10% supplemental talks, I decided in this companion book to closely reverse that; the book includes 95% talks with 5% of meditations. Every so often in the book, you will see a brief meditation (which range from a few seconds to a minute). These meditations will give you an experiential taste of what the HMJ is all about and help you be in the present moment. I hope you enjoy them.

Starting with Chapter 4, each of the following twelve chapters focus on a specific series in the HMJ, except for the final chapter 16.

Contents

Prologue

"We can't solve our problems with the same thinking we used when we created them."

"The people who are crazy enough to think they can change the world are the ones who do."

Albert Einstein

Why Did I Write This Book Now?

Writing this book has taken me on a personal journey of many twists and turns. I had to do a lot of self-exploration in facing up to my intentions and expectations of how my work can help people. It has been a lifelong process of confronting my realities and putting myself out there in the world. It was kind of scary. Why was it scary? Well, if you read Einstein's second quote, you can get some idea. I'm one of those people who is "crazy enough" to think that he can help change the world! If you then go back to Einstein's first quote, it gets serious because I have created one of the most effective tools to change the way people think and problem-solve. It may be one of the most valuable tools we need to get out of the mess we find ourselves in. When you put both of those two things together, you can see why I have some trepidation in writing this down because I begin to sound unrealistic. At the same time, I present myself as a practical, scientifically grounded person with impactful, spiritual experiences. In my case, if you live long enough to make enough mistakes and you are crazy enough to try things that others are too afraid to try, and you are "lucky" enough to experience some unusual spiritual experiences and be with some wonderful people, you might just come up with some great insights that might be valuable.

My Personal Story Leading to an Awakening

When I was nineteen years old and a student at the University of Wisconsin in Madison, I had just returned from a summer of living and working in Manhattan with my girlfriend, Eliza. She was also a student at UW, and we both headed back to school to get ready for the fall semester. I stayed in a little house that I had rented, and Eliza lived with a few other friends nearby. About a month after school started, my persistent learning disability began to act up, making it difficult for me to maintain my studies. Whenever I would start reading my textbooks, the words on the page would dance around like crazy making it very difficult for me to comprehend what I was reading. This was obviously a major handicap, so I wasn't doing well. I had dropped out of school once before because of this issue. Then Eliza came by unexpectedly and announced that she was leaving me for a Brazilian graduate student named Rolando. I was devastated. Rolando was the most handsome man anyone had ever seen. The guy looked like a god. The sight of the two of them walking on campus hand in hand triggered a massive depression, and I became suicidal. I would wake up each morning, go into the kitchen, and pull out the sharpest knife in the drawer to try to cut into my wrists. But fortunately, I failed to do so.

I was also lucky because of the compassion expressed by a close friend, John Zwicky, a graduate student in philosophy. John invited me over for dinner because he knew I was in bad shape. I trudged the mile over to his pad, and he welcomed me into his living room while his girlfriend, Ruth Jacoby, was in the kitchen preparing dinner. As soon as I sat down on his couch, John started telling me about his master's thesis, which described his theory of reality. He stated reality isn't a random series of events; instead, everything is meaningfully related to everything else. There is a oneness to it all. As John gave a long discourse about his thesis, I became enthralled. I absorbed every word, for the reality he described was a world that was evolving with a purpose; there was an intelligent design behind the way the universe was put together. It was much more attractive than the miserable reality I was currently living.

Then a subtle shift started to occur inside of me. I leaned into this new and exciting reality that John was describing. Because I was so desperate, I had nothing holding me back. I was trying to end what I perceived as the meaningless and random life I had been living Then suddenly, a giant flash of light consumed my whole field of view, and the two-hundred-pound weight that had been on my shoulders evaporated. It had been wearing me down, as if to pound me into the ground like a pile driver. Immediately, I felt as light as a feather. I started to laugh uncontrollably being totally elated, feeling free. I was instantly transformed from being massively depressed to being plunged into a state of bliss – all within a fraction of a second. Many years later I concluded that the flash of light was caused by a significant number of neurons in my brain shifted and rewired their connections to adjust to my new perception of reality; it was a case of neuroplasticity on steroids. My spiritual receiver to my Higher Self, which will be discussed more fully later on in this book, became totally active in one fell swoop!

After dinner, I thanked John and Ruth for a fantastic evening. I distinctly remember walking home while light snow was falling and being struck by the beauty of the snowflakes sailing past the streetlights. For the next three weeks, I remained in a constant state of peace and love while being able to go about my business. I went to my classes and felt like I had landed on a new planet. I was experiencing what is called a "beginner's mind," where everything seemed so new and different. I had never seen my world this way before. In fact, I didn't experience a single cognitive thought for those entire three weeks. There was a quiet within me, for my internal processing was being carried out by my Higher Self while my ego-mind went totally silent.

At the end of those three weeks, I was sitting on the edge of my bed, looking out the window, and noticed two students walking by. I was struck by how depressed they looked. And a wave of compassion took me over from my head to my feet. Instantly, I committed right then and there, to start doing something to help people in their struggles. My first vision was to build a heart-based community and to use that as a springboard towards building a better world. I was ready to go and worked constantly towards building that community for the next five months – that was all I did.

Since I was involved in theatre at the time and knew many people in the arts, I decided to start by creating an art community by setting up a cooperative. Soon, I expanded that concept to include everyone in the student community. To provide an organization to support my work, I formed a not-for-profit organization with the name, Open Arts. The main goal of Open Arts was to create love-based events to bring people together to get better organized. We started the first bike-sharing program in the US. During outdoor musical events, students would donate their bikes in the spirit of love while people painted their bikes white. The White Bicycle project had a magical effect on the campus spirit. We then organized a Be-In on Picnic Point along the shores of Lake Mendota, where five thousand students showed up. The event's highlight was an appearance by the poet Alan Ginsburg, who was present, dancing through the crowd playing music with his finger cymbals. The purpose of the Be-In was to celebrate the human spirit, and it was a glorious event. There was a real love movement that was on a roll.

Following that event, ABC television sent five executives to have lunch with me because they wanted me to host a nationally broadcasted television series about the emerging love movement. I was honored but after meditating on this offer, I decided against doing it because I didn't want to commercialize our precious movement with the possibility of compromising its ideals and aspirations for social and political change.

During that amazing spring of 1967, there were many more events, which all led into the famous Summer of Love that same year. However, one afternoon in late May, I was sitting alone, thinking. I realized that people were participating in many events and loving them, but they weren't taking full responsibility to help make things happen. They were just letting things come and go. Too much of the real work was being done by me. Just at that moment, while having this thought, the spirit that had carried me along this whole time left me just as quickly as it had arrived initially. The spirit was gone. It was so sudden I felt like I had fallen down into a deep, dark, empty well and stayed there for a while. It was an excruciating and depressing time for me because everyone expected me to organize the next big thing, and it wasn't going to happen. I no longer had the spirit to give me strength and direction.

Reflections

Reflecting back on this period, my experience demonstrated how powerful a transformative experience can be. However, it appears the intensity of my experience is rare. More likely, your change as you grow spiritually will be more gradual - step by step. Substantive research now shows major changes in consciousness are available to anyone willing to start and maintain a meditation practice which is the main topic of our book. Functional MRI brain images clearly show that our meditation practice has the power to increase and, in some cases, reduce the size of key functional areas of the brain to strengthen the links between the brain and the heart regions to enhance personal development and create strong spiritual connections.

From the time I was nineteen, I have been looking for ways to maintain an enlightened existence for myself and others. Primarily, I explored ways to help our society become transformed through a combination of building beloved communities, action, and spiritual practice.

During all of these experiments, I formed not-for-profit organizations developing peace efforts, embracing the interrelationships between inner peace and world peace here in the States, and then finally in the Middle East. As far as my professional career goes, I started as an eye doctor, which provided for my financial needs and a vehicle to serve people. Later, I became a healthcare venture capitalist, financing and helping run early-stage medical companies focused on improving the delivery of patient care. This experience in business allowed me to live a life of wealth with large homes, big apartments, and luxury vacations around the world. That was nice but not at all spiritually fulfilling.

Through all of this, I was drawn back into getting on with my spiritual journey. After deep introspection and long meditations, the next chapter of my life started to emerge. Through a lot of trial and error, I realized that the best way to contribute to the world was to create a meditation program on a mobile app. Then I realized I needed to develop a comprehensive package of meditation experiences coupled with the related source material. That required me to write this book. I wanted to deliver to you everything you need to succeed. And all of this brought me to where I'm today – a teacher of meditation.

No act of kindness, no matter how small, is ever wasted.

Aesop

Meditation:
Take three gentle breaths and feel a time you expressed deep kindness to someone. As you bring that image into your mind's eye, keep your breathing steady.

Our Big Challenge

At some point for most of us, we discover we are living in an illusion which is making our lives a struggle. We find it out one way or another. Most people uncover it through religious teachings because most major religions teach us that we burden ourselves with a false sense of self. I will refer to this false sense of self in this book as the ego-mind. The ego-mind is a level of our consciousness that has gone amok. It has taken over our awareness so that we believe that the nature of our current consciousness is who we think we are, which we are not. I know for some readers; this sounds a bit crazy. In a lot of ways, it is crazy, but that is our state of Being. Our ego-mind thinks it has a good handle on reality, but it has serious misunderstandings. For starters, it's unable to comprehend nor experience spirit or anything spiritual. It perceives the world from a place of fear while seeing itself separate from the rest of the world. The ego-mind's perspective is why we so often feel alone and isolated. The other characteristic of the ego-mind is that it can't function in the present moment. That is why we spend so much time regretting the past and hoping and fearing a possible future that doesn't exist right now. We are living in an imaginary world – not good!

Luckily, there is a way out of this sad state of affairs. We have a connection to our spiritual essence. That connection is a neural network in our body that functions as a spiritual receiver, just how a radio receiver connects with a radio station so that we can hear the music its broadcasting. Your receiver connects to what I will call here your Higher Self. By the way, your Higher Self is who you are. It's the real you! Another critical factor is that our Higher Self isn't located in our brains. It isn't physical; it resides within the spiritual realm. The challenge is that your spiritual neural network receiver is lying dormant because your ego-mind has been dominating your consciousness your whole life. You need to activate it to connect with your Higher Self and the Universal Spirit. The way you can do that is through meditation. It takes practice but is predictable.

The Higher Self is almost the opposite of the ego-mind. The Higher Self is based upon love, not fear; it feels the spiritual connection with others, the world around us, and with the Universal Spirit. This is all made possible because our Higher Self lives within the present moment where reality takes place.

The HMJ is designed to activate your Higher Self. The first step in meditation is to follow the breath, quiet the ego-mind, and become fully present. This works because, when you get yourself fully in the present moment, the ego-mind immediately goes quiet, and your Higher Self begins to emerge. This is the beginning of the journey. This book and the HMJ are to help us with sorting this all out.

The HMJ Strategy in a Nutshell

The ability to bring to life our dormant receivers is accomplished by activating each of the key components comprising our Higher Self: love, compassion, joy, inner peace, and intuitive wisdom. The strategy is that when you keep activating these key components through meditation, you will start experiencing your Higher Self. I like to refer to these key components as pillars because each one helps "lift and support" your Higher Self experience, so it becomes fully alive, not only while you are meditating but during your waking hours as well. When you can do this while quieting your ego-mind at will for most of your day, this is what I refer to as enlightenment.

In Chapter 3, I provide a good, in-depth overview of the HMJ, and then the rest of the book covers each of the key components: love, compassion, joy, inner peace, intuitive wisdom, plus a lot more! The actual HMJ has twelve series, four hundred meditations comprising one hundred and fifty hours. Each meditation is sequenced to give you maximum effect because it's a carefully designed journey.

Definition of Meditation

Before we describe the benefits one can gain from the HMJ, let's define meditation. The definition of meditation referred to in this book is the technique of quieting the ego-mind to begin experiencing our Higher Self. Our normal waking state which is dominated by the ego-mind generates an electrical brain wave pattern that oscillates at a rate of 15-40 cycles per second called beta waves. When we meditate, our brain waves slow down to 9-14 cycles per second, and these are referred to as alpha waves. When we go into a deeper state of meditation, we generate cycles of between 5-8 per second called theta waves. It is in these slower states where we can do our inner work, which is spiritual in nature.

In meditation, we begin to follow the breath to allow the mind to focus inwardly while still being awake and alert. We are not concentrating on the external world or the events taking place around us. Meditation requires an inner state that is still and highly focused, helping the cognitive mind become silent and our Higher Self to be fully present.

The Benefits of the Journey

Here is a list of some of the experiential benefits the *HappCo Meditation Journey* mobile app provides. It's a way for you to:
1. Establish a strong mind/body connection.
2. Learn to quiet the ego-mind consistently.
3. Meditate on the following to help connect with your Higher Self:
    a. Love
    b. Compassion
    c. Joy
    d. Inner peace
    e. Intuitive wisdom
4. Rewire and process your emotional hotspots to increase your level of equanimity.
5. Temper the negative tones of your inner voices.
6. Become spiritually connected.
7. Attain enlightenment.

Timing and Synchronicity

The release of this book now is significant because, as they say, "timing is everything." We need to think differently for our species to survive, then meditation programs that can help people experience enlightenment should be a hot commodity. I believe that we are on a survival track, admittedly a precarious one at the current time, but what is emerging are things that we need to do to land on our feet. One thing we need more than anything else is breakthrough meditation experiences. That is why I feel compelled to present the *HappCo Meditation Journey* and this accompanying handbook, *Embracing Your Higher Self*. I'm proud to present it to you, and hopefully, it can help in our collective work that needs doing.

1

Making Some Sense of the Spirit World

Before we get into exploring and defining enlightenment in greater detail, let's explore the spirit world a bit to get ourselves oriented and create the context within which enlightenment emerges. This is essential because the *HappCo Meditation Journey* is a spiritual quest.

There are spiritual forces that affect us beyond our physical bodies, and it's valuable to acknowledge that they exist and try to make sense of them without adhering to a specific religious teaching or, on the other hand, tossing the whole spiritual idea out the window. These are some of the key objectives for writing this book.

The Definition of Spirit

First, let's initially clarify the meanings of spirit, spiritual, religious, religion, and secular. There is confusion around these words, that we should start off clarifying them to minimize further misunderstandings. According to *Webster's Dictionary*[2], the spirit's: *an animating or vital principle held to give life to physical organisms* – referring to the spirit of life. Spiritual is defined as: *of, relating to, consisting of, or affecting the spirit* and, according to one definition, the spirit's *concerned with religious values*. In turn, religious is defined in two ways: 1. *relating to or manifesting faithful devotion to an acknowledged ultimate reality or deity*. 2. *Of, relating to, or devoted to religious beliefs or observances*. And finally, religion is defined as *the service and worship of God or the supernatural*.

For our work, spiritual relates to the animating, vital principle or force that gives life to our physical bodies. According to this definition of the spirit, the spirit's fully compatible with a secular viewpoint, where secular is defined by being *not overtly or specifically religious*. That is a viewpoint that isn't associated with a particular religious teaching or institution. Some definitions of secular imply referring to things nonspiritual, but that isn't the definition of secular we are considering here.

Combining Experiential and Cognitive

The HMJ's experiences provide guidance and pointers along the way. This guidance is key to a successful venture. If we are unsure of the context and contours within which we travel, that uncertainty can negatively affect the quality of our experiences and how far we can go. A crucial part of achieving enlightenment is eventually having aha moments generated by combining cognitive and experiential ingredients. That is why we possess both capabilities. The primary experiential part is available to you in the meditation experiences available on the HMJ. The cognitive explorations into the world of spirit and what the HMJ is all about are available here in this book.

The Varying Interpretations of God and the Universal Spirit

As far as the issue of God is concerned, there is a broad spectrum of interpretations about what is universal spirit. Most Western religions (Christian, Jewish, and Muslim) perceive God as the unifying energy of the universe and the creator. In Eastern religions, Hindus have their main God, Brahman, who is worshipped mainly through three gods: Brahma, a creator of the universe; Vishnu, a preserver of the universe; and Shiva, a destroyer of the universe. Buddhists believe in a significant unifying spirit but not a creator of the universe.

Sorting Out the Spirit World From the Physical World

We all thirst for simple explanations in trying to make sense of the spirit world. In many organized religions, the descriptions of the spirit world vis-a-vis the physical world can be pretty confusing. I believe the confusion stems from the many people through millennia contributing to the writing of their holy books, commentaries, religious ceremonies, and traditions. The significance of these inconsistencies hit home for me a few years ago, when the host of one of my Passover dinners announced there might not be reliable historical records to substantiate the story of Exodus in the Torah. The Jews were reportedly freed from slavery in Egypt while helping build the pyramids!

I grew up as the youngest child in my family and had the honor of reading the Four Questions in Hebrew during the Seder ceremony. Passover is my favorite annual spiritual event. It's a time to celebrate our desire for all people in the world to become free. I always looked forward to the celebration, and I still do because of the feeling of love and compassion that surrounds this beautiful tradition. But, to think that the Exodus may only be a story was quite traumatic! Growing up, I was told it was true. There was always the question and the endless debates of how the Red Sea opened up for the Jews who had just been set free by the Egyptian pharaoh lead by Moses. This miraculous escape occurred after the Egyptians had suffered terribly, enduring the ten plagues God brought down upon them to convince the pharaoh to let the Jews go. The other persistent question was how the Red Sea swallowed up the Egyptian army as they were trying to recapture the fleeing Jews right after the pharaoh changed his mind about freeing them. I was in awe, watching Charlton Heston play Moses on the big screen. I was proud of being a part of a people who'd experienced this amazing history of miracles.

Over the past few years, I have been stewing over this uncertainty. Luckily my brother, Gene, working with me on editing this book, referred me to an interview with Richard Elliott Friedman, professor of Jewish Studies at the University of Georgia. He explained where the confusion occurred and made a strong argument that the Exodus did take place![3] It was such a relief that I no longer had to live with this disappointment. I could now bring back those fond memories of Heston bringing down the commandments from Mt. Sinai, in peace.

God, Universal Spirit or Source

From here on out, I will be using the word God to refer to a Universal Spirit or Source. Some people feel uncomfortable with the use of the word *God* because of the many images that are associated with the word. But, after finishing writing this book, I decided I couldn't get away from the word. I'm attached to it and will be using it throughout the book. If you feel comfortable with the words Universal Spirit or Source or some other word or image, feel free to think about that word, idea, or feeling you have when you see the word God.

I believe in one God who is the creator and is at our core and comprises our essence. However, the value of this book and the meditation program will still be valuable to you, regardless of your belief system about God or individual spirit. In addition, for me, God is formless, based solely upon my personal experiences. I have experienced God as a vast, infinite spirit possessing love, compassion, joy, peace, and infinite wisdom. These are the same basic elements that comprise our Higher Self.

From Our Physical Body to Our Higher Self to God

I believe that the relationship between the physical body, the Higher Self and God, is a smooth, uninterrupted spiritual continuum. The body is infused with spirit. The Higher Self provides spiritual energy and consciousness to our physical bodies. Our Higher

Self has some form to it that correlates with our bodies. The Higher Self also provides a bridge to God. The key differentiator between God and our Higher Self is that God is infinite and formless and focuses on the whole universe. This simple structure allows us to feel free to connect with God any time we want. Having this open-door policy is a key foundation to living a healthy and happy life.

Here is the first brief meditation with your eyes open though you can do it with your eyes closed if you prefer. I highly recommend you do all of the brief meditations because you will experience this book more deeply and better understand its meaning. They only take a few moments! For this meditation, let's do a simple breathing exercise:

> **Meditation:**
> I invite you to stop for a moment to take three deep, gentle breaths while observing the air going through your nose as you inhale and going out of your nose as you exhale.

The Formless Debate

Again, I believe that the Higher Self possesses a spiritual form, while our bodies are filled with spirit taking on a physical form. It makes sense then that our physical bodies are the way they are because of God's efforts and the constraints of the laws of the universe (evolution, gravity, atomic structures, time-space, and so on).

Some spiritual teachers believe the Higher Self doesn't have any "form" because spirit, in general, isn't physical. When you read on, you will see why I don't buy this argument.

For further clarification, the words soul and spirit are often used interchangeably. However, when I use the word *spirit*, I do as a general term for the spiritual realm that includes any mind-related entities, including the ego-mind, the Higher Self, and God. I only use the word soul when referring to the Higher Self because I believe the soul and the Higher Self are identical.

The Higher Self (Soul) Operating Separately From the Body

Looking back on my experiences, I have had two events and one ongoing life experience that frame my conclusions on the Higher Self having a form and living longer than our bodies do. The first was years ago when I had an out-of-body experience when I found myself floating near the ceiling of an examination room in my dentist's office while being given nitrous oxide gas before having my cavities filled to avoid feeling pain. While floating near the ceiling, I was able to look down at my body in the dental chair. I was aware and fully conscious, plus I sensed I had a form, not necessarily with arms and legs, but I felt whole.

Dr. Zach

The other profound moment was when I was at the funeral of a close friend's granddaughter. My close friend, George Simon, had died a few years before his granddaughter's tragic death due to an automobile accident. While I was kneeling to observe her in an open coffin before the formal funeral ceremony, I looked up, and there was George's spirit, floating above her body, incomplete form, grabbing onto his granddaughter's arm, seemingly pulling her up to him. It was a vivid experience. I didn't have much time to continue observing this happening because there was a long line behind me. Later that day, at a family luncheon, I mentioned what I experienced to a number of the family members, and George's oldest daughter said that she had seen George as well.

Between these two experiences, I became a firm believer in the presence of a soul that is different from God because I experienced my soul and George's soul having form, albeit in a spiritual form. My significant lifelong experience is that as I get older, my observing consciousness doesn't seem to age but does grow wiser. It appears to be operating from a different time frame relative to the body. Because of this differential, I believe in reincarnation – that our souls use the body we have now and, when this body becomes used up, our souls leave this body and eventually take on a new one. It makes sense to me that the lifetime of our souls is much greater than the lifetime of each of the bodies we use. We need a number of bodies to live a full "soul's life." How many bodies a soul uses is a question I can't answer, and how enlightenment affects this process, I also don't know. In Buddhism and Hinduism, enlightenment plays a big role in reincarnation, and each religion has different beliefs around this dynamic.

Are We All One?

Now, one of the challenges we face is understanding how we are connected. When our consciousness sticks to our ego-minds, we experience a sharp separateness between ourselves and everyone else, including our immediate family members. Our ego-minds primarily focus on each of us having individual bodies because the ego-mind can't experience spiritual reality and interconnectedness. From a spiritual perspective, if you believe we emerge from the one God, then at the deepest level of existence, we are all connected. And if you take it a step further, from a holistic perspective, we are all one.

A Theory of a Grand Design

The previous discussion assumes that God is formless, is the creator of life and the entire physical universe. It then seems logical to think God values physical experiences because God created us in a physical form and allowed us to experience life, our Higher Self, and God from the vantage point of this material world. To differentiate the human race from all other creatures on Earth, humans possess a sophisticated ability to self-reflect, to be aware that we are aware. This self-reflection capability is maybe what God needs from us - to be continually *self-aware*. In other words,

God needs a human mirror to reflect upon itself and for us to reflect upon our true selves by the way we live our lives. This requires the attainment of enlightenment. Maybe that is the grand design, if there is one.

To appreciate all of this and have hope that there might be a grand design, one has to look at the tremendous amount of creativity and billions of years of "work" needed to manifest us, which is in and of itself a miracle. Concerning God's work, I refer to the extraordinary processes of creating life out of inanimate molecules, creating a vast library of information in each cell's DNA. In addition, making the mitosis process by which cells duplicate themselves thereby manifests multicellular creatures; and the myriad of species that go through evolution to finally get to us.

> **Meditation:**
> I invite you to stop for a moment and take three gentle deep breaths while concentrating on the part of your consciousness that is being aware of your breath. Now take three more gentle breaths and then relax.

The Two Major Illusions to Dispel

Our spiritual journey is discovering and connecting with our true reality, and this requires us to dispel two major illusions to reach a state of enlightenment. One is dealing with the ego-mind having fooled us into thinking it's who we really are. The second related illusion is thinking we are solely our bodies, thoughts, sensations, and feelings separate us from our world. Experiencing both of these illusions is like being lost in a spiritual desert, searching for drinking water. When we look around, all we see is sand as far as the eye can see. The search ahead requires a combination of cognitive and experiential skills. The cognitive abilities serve as a GPS function to find out where we need to drill. Then, once we are properly situated, we can experientially drill down within ourselves, using a meditation practice to connect with our vast spiritual reservoir to quench our thirst.

Being in This World But Not of It

We are living in this physical world, but it's key to develop an awareness of observing our daily lives from a spiritual perspective. A good guideline in life is to be in this physical world but not of it. Jesus made this point clear.[4] An excellent way to keep an arm's length distance in dealing with the physical world is to no longer identify with your body, emphasizing that the body isn't all that we are. From the ego-mind's perspective, it believes we are only physical bodies, and our happiness resides in having material things and possessions. "The more I have, the happier I will be." That is true about other things like sex, recreational drugs, and power over people. However, there are many stories of people who wake up one day and realize that, after spending a lot of their lives amassing wealth and power, this isn't the way to happiness. That happened to me as well. In Chapter 5, I propose a definition of true happiness based upon breaking free from the illusion of the ego-mind while bringing to life our Higher Self, independent from physical possessions.

No Longer Believe You Are Your Body But Still Honor It

Let's examine this question: what role do our bodies play in life? It makes sense that our bodies serve as tools for our formless God because God created us. Otherwise, why would there be a need for our physical bodies? The full spectrum from God to the Higher Self to the physical body is along a spiritual continuum, moving from pure formlessness to a form configuration. The role our Higher Self plays is a bridge between the formless God and the physical body. However, I want to clarify that the physical body is form, heavily infused with spirit. The body uses our spiritual energy for organization and function. This concept became evident when I observed several graphical video conceptions of what is going on inside our cells. The complexity is overwhelming and what became clear is that the activity in our bodies isn't all about chemistry and physics but primarily spiritual forces at work, mainly in the form of consciousness, which is our life force in action. Consciousness is a spiritual, self-organizing entity not only for our minds but for our bodies as well.[5] Therefore, our bodies are made of spiritual and physical elements – together, they are one. On a larger dimension, every person is created by God, all part of the one.

Q. Are We Form or Formless?

God is a spiritual entity that created the physical world, which we define as the world of form. The spirit world, which is different from the physical world, we define as the world of formlessness. If you accept this premise then, we are formless at our ultimate core, where we are one with God. Could this be true? Yes. Why is this relevant? We are dealing with a few challenges in trying to understand what we are made of fully. If we are at our core sourced from a formless God, and our Higher Self has a spiritual form, and our bodies are physical form, are we creatures of form or formlessness?

I believe we are both. We are part of a continuum from formlessness to form. To further make this lack of distinction between formlessness and form clearer, the latest in scientific discourses ponder the essential nature of the atom, which is the building block of form. When you explore deep into the atom, you discover subatomic particles which are much smaller than protons and neutrons, such as quarks and neutrinos. Quantum physicists now question if there is actually form at the atom's core or only formlessness and probabilities?[6] Top theoretical scientists are trying to grapple with these uncertainties, and one thing is clear: physical form isn't what we generally think it to be.

Einstein's theory of general relativity clarified that physical reality is quite pliable and so much a function of our perceptions and circumstances. For example, if you are traveling at the speed of light, time stands still. Time stops and, as you slow down, time speeds up. Quantum mechanics takes the uncertainty of physical reality to even more bizarre levels. To assume we understand the world of form as being this solid, well-understood state is an illusion.

Emptiness or Love?

Many of the leading Eastern religions use the words emptiness, unmanifested and formless to describe the spiritual realm. I'm not crazy about their usage because they use words that are hard to wrap our minds around. In our journey, we are going to take the opposite approach. Instead of looking at the spiritual realm as incomprehensible, we will approach it directly from our feelings when we experience spirit. I agree that the cognitive mind has its limits in comprehending spirit, so the experiences we have in meditation are essential. But, if consciousness is who we are, then the feelings we have when we experience spirit should be how we define spirit: love, compassion, joy, inner peace, and intuitive wisdom all in one package. Learning how to experience spirit through heightening our ability to experience each of the key components of spirit (Higher Self and God) through the HMJ is the ticket to enlightenment.

Scientists' Sense of the Relationships between Spirit and Form

We tend to think that scientists focus on the physical world and have no patience or interest in the spiritual realm. However, Einstein, the greatest scientist in history, looked at reality from a spiritual perspective, which was reflected in the following two quotes: "I want to know God's thoughts, the rest are details;" and then he wrote, "[A scientists'] religious feeling takes the form of a rapturous amazement at the harmony of natural law, which reveals an intelligence of such superiority…"[7] Einstein expressed the relationship he and other scientists have with understanding the nature of physical reality in scientific and mathematical terms. He perceived a universal spirit or God-like, intelligent entity creating it all from the scientific perspective.

Max Planck, considered the father of quantum mechanics, even though a team of scientists contributed to its entire formulation, believed that the mind is more essential than matter. "I regard consciousness as fundamental. I regard matter as derivative from consciousness. Everything that we talk about, everything that we regard as existing, postulates consciousness."[8]

The two most significant scientific breakthroughs that best describe the nature of reality are Einstein's general theory of relativity and Planck's quantum mechanics. The fathers of these theories believed in a spirit or consciousness as the underlying basis of physical reality. Then why did the scientific world end up being so spiritually vacuous? That is a great question.

During the Age of Reason or the Enlightenment period, scientists created a body of knowledge that was diametrically opposed to the then-current societal beliefs, which religious institutions dominated. As science was discovering new scientific breakthroughs that were disproving spiritual beliefs, many segments of society were quickly adopting these new visions of reality. The best example of this is Darwin's theory of evolution.

The lay press promoted Darwin's theory. Behind the scenes, Darwin's theories were refuted by the most outstanding paleontologist of the time, Louis Agassiz, a professor at Harvard. Darwin sent one of his final draft copies of his book, *On the Origin of Species,* to Agassiz for feedback. Agassiz refuted Darwin's theory for several reasons: "a scientific mistake, untrue in its facts, unscientific in its methods, and mischievous in its tendencies."[9] One primary reason for Agassiz's dismay was that Darwin didn't fully address the most "troubling anomaly," the Cambrian explosion.

The Cambrian explosion, a fossil discovery, represents a period starting 500 million years ago that lasted about 20 million years. This discovery showcased so many new and diverse species of life in such a short period that Darwin's theory couldn't even begin to explain it. Even Darwin admitted that this discovery tested his theories' validity and hoped that future findings would help validate his theory. During the past 150 years, there have been no new supportive fossil discoveries to help to substantiate Darwin's theory.

Over the past century and one-half, Darwin's theories have been under constant attacks and criticism. Forty years ago, Stephen Jay Gould, another famous Harvard paleontologist, declared that Neo-Darwinism "is effectively dead, despite its persistence as textbook orthodoxy." Gould had his own theory of evolution that was described as *punctuated equilibrium*. That species undergo long periods of stasis followed by rapid changes over relatively short periods instead of continuously accumulating slow changes over millions of years, as Darwin had theorized.[10] More recently, as a greater understanding of the complexities of how genes function, Darwin's theories are now only seriously being considered to explain minor physical changes but not to explain the emergence of new species.

The most fascinating discussion is in the field of intelligent design and how it might play a role in evolution. Two books that I've just finished reading are *Darwin's Doubts; the Explosive Origin of Animal Life and the Case for Intelligent Design*[11], and the *Signature in the Cell; DNA Evidence for Intelligent Design*[12] by Stephen Meyer. I highly recommend reading them both.

Stephen Meyer received his doctorate at Cambridge University, and his dissertation was on the origin of life biology. What is so fascinating is that we have here a credible research scientist whose life work has been on how the spirit plays an active role in the origin of life and the evolution of life. The big takeaway for me is that when you analyze the complexities of how life begins and how new species are created, random mutation and natural selection are only a small part of the factors involved. I believe that our spirit and consciousness actively infuse our physical bodies, managing our creation, moment-to-moment functioning, and evolutionary direction. Meyer's book validated my belief.

Where Are We Headed?

I discern an overall pattern to the spiritual game plan that runs parallel to the role we as individuals play in providing a self-reflective function by serving God. We periodically discuss the role that each of our struggles play in motivating us to reach out beyond the ego-minds' nonspiritual perspective to search for greater meaning - and that this search often ends up with us discovering spirit. As our planet and our species currently face existential dangers, our collective struggles create a dangerous pressure cooker environment. This forces us to try and figure out how we can elevate our consciousness to create a new, more healing environment that's different from the current one. The fact is that we may not be able to survive if we continue on the path that we are on.

I describe in this book that in our brains and hearts, we possess a neural network that is currently dormant, which is the receiver for our Higher Self and God. God has, through evolution, provided us with these receivers to experience our Higher Self as well as God. If enough of the human species takes this spiritual journey, creating heaven on Earth is a real possibility and maybe where we are all headed if things go our way.

Is this the holy grail? The first major story in the Bible depicts human beings in a state of enlightenment in the Garden of Eden. Then we lose it by falling into a realm of illusion, dominated by our ego-mind based on fear. It now appears that God is moving us towards a world filled with humans who are rediscovering the truth and connecting with the spirit all day long. This seems to be the biggest story of all time! That is why I feel that this book and the app, the *HappCo Meditation Journey,* are so relevant, not only for individual growth but for the whole human journey.

Meditation:
I invite you now to be in the here and now by taking three deep, gentle breaths through your nose while feeling the cool air coming in and the warm air coming out.

2

What is
Enlightenment?

Embracing Your Higher Self

To know yourself as the Being underneath the thinker, the stillness underneath the mental noise, the love and joy underneath the pain, is freedom, salvation, enlightenment.

Eckhart Tolle, The Power of Now[13]

To enjoy good health, to bring true happiness to one's family, to bring peace to all, one must first discipline and control one's own mind. If a man can control his mind, he can find the way to enlightenment, all wisdom and virtue will naturally come to him.

Gautama Buddha[14]

The search for enlightenment is alive and well; it's the primary purpose of a good percentage of today's serious meditators. We all want a transformation in our lives, how we experience life, and possess a level of happiness and meaning that is spiritually fulfilling.

Most major spiritual traditions agree that humankind has been in a fog - living an illusion. The source of this illusion is our ego-mind at some point in our evolution, expanded its role beyond its primary job of taking care of our earthly needs, protecting our bodies, and passing along our genes. The ego-mind evolved so that we became disoriented, thinking our ego-mind is who we are when defining ourselves. This development was incredibly significant because we

55

went from a love-based consciousness to a fear-based one. When this confusion occurred, the consciousness that represented our Higher Self became overpowered by the ego-mind and went to "sleep," if you will. This development was a disaster because the role of our Higher Self is to collectively help us run our lives here on Earth and keep us connected to spirit and with God. Luckily, the core wiring for the receivers in our brain and our hearts are tuned to our Higher Self still exist in the form of neural networks that are just waiting for us to bring them back to life; it's in a dormant state now. This book will teach you in detail the HMJ's approach and why it's effective in reenergizing this essential spiritual receiver.

Our Definition of Enlightenment

Enlightenment is defined in this book as the ability to sustain your Higher Self for most of your waking hours while assigning and maintaining your ego-mind to the role of servant. When you experience your Higher Self, you become in touch with God. A crucial part of your spiritual journey is allowing your Higher Self to emerge and dominate your everyday consciousness. This process includes acknowledging that your ego-mind, which is currently dominating your consciousness, isn't your Higher Self but an illusory sense of self. To successfully take on this challenge requires a few skills. Those skills include:

1. Quieting the ego-mind through the use of several tools, including staying fully present.

2. Learning to experience the five key spiritual characteristics that comprise your Higher Self.
3. Bringing to life the dormant receiver for your Higher Self to allow it into your everyday experience.
4. Learning to connect with God with love.
5. Creating and maintaining a practice of meditation.

All of the above require a consistent meditation habit. Without meditation, all of the things you will be reading about will be an excellent intellectual exercise, but that isn't the book's purpose.

What Do We Mean By the Ego-mind?

Before we go any further, I want to clarify the difference between the ego-mind and the ego. This book refers to the ego-mind extensively, and the ego-mind is different from what Freud or modern psychology defines the ego to be. In our standard reference to ego, we usually refer to how highly one thinks of oneself – sometimes in a negative way: "He has a big ego."

Freud developed a tripartite model of the mind that included the ego, the id, and the superego.[15] Freud defined the ego's function to manage sexual and aggressive impulses while navigating the tensions between those impulses and the pressures and values of society. In modern psychology, the ego is the self-consciousness system.[16] The self-consciousness system narrates a portion of human consciousness that reflects one's thoughts, feelings, and actions and inhibits or legitimizes them to oneself and others.

For our work and discussions, the ego-mind is this self-consciousness system functions in a state of illusion. It's living in the past and future, not in the present moment, based on fear compared to our Higher Self, which is based on love. The ego-mind considers itself your Higher Self, but in actuality, it isn't. The ego-mind isn't even aware that a true Higher Self exists. It neither understands nor cares about this confusion. It's programmed to dominate our consciousness and stay dominant. Freud and modern psychology do not acknowledge this interpretation of how the mind works because their school of thought doesn't consider the spiritual component of reality.[17] Thus, they don't at all identify the existence of the Higher Self.

The discovery of the illusion of the ego-mind goes back to Buddha 2,500 years ago and has been studied experientially by generations of monks and gurus ever since. The acknowledgment of this core illusion dilemma isn't solely limited to Buddhists. It permeates the teachings of most major religions.

Quieting the Ego-mind

One of the essential skills needed in almost all meditation practices is the ability to quiet the ego-mind. This skill is most effective when following the breath for extended periods. It's difficult because the ego-mind will consistently intrude, and the ability to reduce its intrusion requires practice and focus.

When you follow your breath, your ego-mind goes quiet. That is a significant occurrence. Why is that? Because the ego-mind, which is an illusory sense of self, can't function at all in the present moment. To clarify, I don't mean that your ego isn't working. I mean, your *ego-mind*, that part of the ego with an illusory sense of self, can't function. To further clarify, the ego-mind is a subset of the ego.

The ego-mind can only exist in an imaginary world. That imaginary world is in the past and the future but not in the here and now. That is why we spend so much time regretting past events and anticipating future ones because it's the only arena the ego-mind can play in. The ego-mind's constantly thinking of the past and future which is all the ego-mind is capable of doing. We aren't thinking these things because we feel these thoughts are essential. We do it because we are stuck in the past and future. Another big question is, why would our minds spend so much time in the past and the future when we have available to us the present moment? The present moment is the only "time zone" where we can experience our thoughts, emotions, bodily sensations, perceptions, and moods. For what reason would we want to be cut off from, basically, our reality?

For the ego-mind to function, it needs to stay away from reality – the here and now – and it desperately needs to push us away from the present moment dominating our consciousness. It functions as a separate being. It forcefully directs our awareness to keep us from the present moment. It's also the key reason why people resist meditating because the ego-mind doesn't want to be found out and give up control.

Let's go through this a bit more systematically so we can get this straight. If you accept that reality only exists within the here and now, then something that can't function in the present moment must not be real. Correct? So, we must then conclude that the ego-mind's sense of self is an illusion; it doesn't represent our authentic selves! If it did, it would not become silent when we are in the present moment where reality resides. This proof is straightforward. If this is the first time you are getting this straight, I know it might be a bit mind-blowing. People are waking up to this fact, and it may be why meditation is becoming so popular.

With humanity in this great state of confusion, our conscious awareness is struggling, and we have our work cut out for us to bring us back to reality. This handbook is going to help us with sorting out some of this dilemma.

What Does Enlightenment Feel Like?

The best way I can describe what enlightenment feels like is by mentioning the five fundamental pillars of the Higher Self. They are love, compassion, joy, inner peace, and intuitive wisdom. If you experience all of these key spiritual characteristics simultaneously, you will feel what enlightenment is all about. It feels glorious and makes your whole body vibrate! That is what you learn to do on the journey. I compare it to playing five individual notes comprising a beautiful-sounding chord. When you play each note one at a time and savor their sounds, you say, "That is so cool!" If I then ask you to play all five at the same time and you've never done that before, you might ask, "Is that going to work?" Well, when you do it, and the sound of that chord rings out into the room, you might exclaim, "WOW!" That is what learning to experience enlightenment is all about, and that is what this book is all about.

> **Meditation:**
> I invite you to take three deep gentle breaths, while placing your awareness on your heart region. As you inhale, make believe your heart is breathing in and as you exhale imagine your heart is breathing out. Please do that three times.

Does Enlightenment Come and Go?

One significant clarification is that enlightenment isn't an altered state that just quickly comes and goes. When you become enlightened, you keep reaching new and higher plateaus as you continually grow throughout your life. There will inevitably be times of regression that heavy emotional traumas will cause. Life for all of us, no matter what state of mind we are in, is always a process of expansion and contraction. One essential truth in life is that nothing stays the same, and enlightenment isn't a static experience - it's dynamic. The main difference is that you become rooted within the spiritual realm while simultaneously being engaged with the physical world. When you live life in the present moment, your sensory experiences become vibrant and alive.

The best way to look at the HMJ is that it's a path that you take while being connected to your Higher Self, traveling from the surface of your consciousness, going down through your subconscious, moving deeper within yourself, going further along, until you connect with God. This journey is facilitated by learning and experiencing the spiritual characteristics of the Higher Self, which are the same as the ones for enlightenment.

Q: Why Is Enlightenment Such a Rare Occurrence?

Even though enlightenment has historically been rare, it's an achievable goal if you have the right strategies and practice. Because it has been so rare, many people feel it's an idealized vision of what a person can achieve and is unattainable. The fact that it's such a rare event can understandably support this view. However, what we describe in this book is a clear step-by-step pathway to achieving enlightenment that will facilitate it becoming a common one.

Enlightenment has been so rare because the strategies and techniques applied in the Eastern wisdom traditions are so physically and mentally intense – such as physical isolation, strict discipline, and pain – that many people don't want to commit to this type of extreme sacrifice. However, severe pain, for example, isn't a requirement for emotional and spiritual growth, even though the process of struggle does facilitate moving you along on your journey. This book is a practical guide to help you achieve enlightenment without having to go through such ordeals.

The "No Self" Towards Enlightenment

The Buddha taught that we don't have an authentic self and that part of the process of becoming enlightened is to meditate on having "no self." This practice can then free one up from all suffering to experience enlightenment. This topic is controversial, and I must address it because I had a misunderstanding concerning this issue for a long time. I thought that his teaching of "no self" was to dis-identify with the ego-mind. It was a shock to me that he was saying that when you fully dis-identify you have no self, not even a Higher Self! I have great difficulty in fully understanding how a path to enlightenment is achieved this way. From the writings on Buddha's teachings, there seemed to be some confusion about this issue – if there is no self, then who or what is being aware when you finally quiet the ego-mind?

Dr. Zach

In Robert Wright's Book, entitled *Why Buddhism is True,* he has an excellent section in his Chapter 5,[18] questioning the logic of the discourse Buddha had with five monks about how to become enlightened by letting go of the sense of self. There is a lot of confusion concerning this particular discourse because the Buddha is not very clear. After you let go of self to become free of cravings and aversions, including letting go of your consciousness, what part of you is left to be aware moment to moment so you can function in this world. Wright states: [19]

> *But this landmark argument that the self doesn't exist has one odd feature: an occasional tendency to suggest that the self exists. Near the end of the discourse, delivering the take-home lesson, the Buddha instructs the monks to go through each of the aggregates and say, "This isn't mine, this I'm not, this isn't myself." He says that a monk who follows this guidance unswervingly "becomes passion-free. In his freedom from passion, he is emancipated." Okay, fine. But if there's no self, then what is the nature of the "he" that is liberated after all the things that aren't self have been disowned? Who is doing the disowning? If you don't exist, then how can you say of each aggregate, "This isn't mine, this I'm not"? If it makes sense to say that there's something you don't possess and that there's something you aren't, then there must be a you in the first place, right?*

How can the Buddha, on the one hand, insist that the self doesn't exist, and, on the other hand, keep using terms like I and you and he and she?

To be clear, nothing was written down describing Buddha's talks until two hundred years after his death, so a lot might have been lost in the translation between the time he gave the actual talks and the written record. Wright clearly states that the written records of what Buddha believed about the self are unclear, and there are many differing interpretations.

Dr. Robert A.V. Thurman, professor of religion at Columbia University and a former Buddhist monk, helped make sense out of Buddha's "no self" statements by remarking that "the Buddha said, 'We don't exist,' to shock us. He meant to say that we don't exist in the way we think we exist, that is what he meant … our egocentrism is based upon an illusion, a miswiring in the core of our programming … that there was a way of Being, a relational being. A pure nexus of relationships totally interconnected with all of beings, not being really different than the universe…that ultimate unity and relational differences [are] simultaneously present and that made the Buddha really happy. That is why he is smiling in a lot of his statues. That is all that enlightenment is – being connected, realizing the interconnectedness with all things and all beings viscerally – realizing that is what enlightenment is. It isn't mysterious. Isn't it simple?"[20]
[21]

Dr. Zach

What is spiritual realization? The belief that you are spirit? No, that's a thought. A little closer to the truth than the thought that believes you are who your birth certificate says you are, but still a thought. Spiritual realization is to see clearly that what I perceive, experience, think, or feel is ultimately not who I am, that I cannnot find myself in all those things that continuously pass away. The Buddha was probably the first human being to see this clearly, and so anata (no self) became one of the central points of his teaching. And when Jesus said, "Deny thyself," what he meant was: Negate (and thus undo) the illusion of self. If the self – ego – were truly who I am, it would be absurd to "deny" it. What remains is the light of consciousness in which perceptions, experiences, thoughts, and feelings come and go. That is Being, that is the deeper, true I. When I know myself as that, whatever happens in my life is no longer of absolute but only of relative importance. I honor it, but it loses its absolute seriousness, its heaviness. The only thing that ultimately matters is this: Can I sense my essential Beingness, the I'm, in the background of my life at all times? To be more accurate, can I sense the I am that I am at this moment?

Tolle is referring to the Higher Self when he mentions the words "light of consciousness," "Being," "true I," "essential Beingness" and the "I am."

So, it appears that Wright, Robert Thurman, and Tolle all indicate there is a Higher Self consciousness available to us after we dispel the imaginary sense of self the ego-mind has created. The conception of a "no self" is confusing and maybe a roadblock on the journey to enlightenment.

> **Meditation:**
> I invite you to take three deep, gentle breaths and observe the cool air going into your nose as you inhale and the warm air going out your nose as you exhale.

Is Our Species Destined to Become Enlightened?

What is exciting is that we all are on this journey to Embracing Your Higher Self together. Each of us is being pushed along towards an awakening. We keep getting spiritual messages and whispers trying to guide us, and it's our responsibility to start listening. If you are already attending, you might need to hear a little more intently - become a bit more conscious. Now that you are reading this book, you get closer to being aware of a highly effective program that can lead you towards enlightenment. I hope you read on in this book and decide to start taking the HMJ to help move you along on your journey.

Can Enlightenment Occur Spontaneously?

In Chapter 9, I describe my awakening spontaneously occurring without any prior meditation practice, proving we all have the receivers in place to experience enlightenment. We need only to motivate ourselves to, as the Nike tagline urged us on, "Just do it!" Creating an actual Age of Enlightenment is no longer beyond hope. It's about actively transforming our consciousness by moving our ground of awareness from fear back to love and changing the world.

Enlightenment and Ethics

Before we go further, I want to address the question of how an enlightened person behaves. Nobody is perfect. We may be perfect on one level and not on another. Living our lives and learning how to behave is a process of contraction, expansion, growing, making mistakes, and learning from those mistakes. That process is always ongoing. To be enlightened is to be tapped into the same facilities available to us but on a higher, spiritual level. Many times, people give enlightened souls unrealistic expectations. The truth is that we are all human beings with our strengths and weaknesses. Tapping into our Higher Self gives us great tools and facilities to live our lives from our hearts with deep love and compassion, but it doesn't make us perfect.

Q: Can the experience of enlightenment eliminate the ego?

Being able to eliminate the ego brings up a sensitive issue for some people, but an enlightened person isn't supernatural. Being connected with the spirit and overcoming the illusion of the ego-mind doesn't mean eliminating the ego. The ego is deeply rooted within the functioning of the brain, well down into the brainstem. To have the ability to short circuit that wiring and cut it off from a person's consciousness is to me unfathomable. It's essential for the health and future of our species that the experience of enlightenment is made available and perceived as achievable for all people. This realization is critical for people to know they are not wasting their time working towards attaining enlightenment.

> **Meditation:**
> I invite you take three gentle breaths while you breathe in a sense of relaxation and breathe out tension in your body.

3

Embracing Your Higher Self

Nothing Like Scientific Proof

The practice of meditation started to become widely accepted within the scientific community when Dr. Richard Davidson, Antoine Lutz, and Mathieu Ricard published their EEG and functional MRI ("fMRI") studies, starting in 2003.[22]

Their fMRI images clearly showed the differences in the size of various functional parts of the brain of experienced meditators compared to non-meditators. Their measurements of the brain's electrical signals and blood flow revealed how meditation could alter the size of significant functional components of the brain. Researchers and the public were able to see for themselves the resultant structural changes in the brain. Meditation moved from being a fringe practice to one with serious and important ramifications. Later studies demonstrated its value in one's personal life and the world of business. Many studies now show that meditation affects the function and structure of the brain to improve one's ability to live a happier and healthier life and a more loving and productive one.

Strategies and Tactics in the HappCo Meditation Journey

This chapter explores the strategies and tactics used in designing the *HappCo Meditation Journey*. I serve as your guide and one of the coaches in assisting participants on this journey. The HMJ is designed to be consistent, effective, and engaging. It contains an ever-growing library of audio meditations for your practice. It currently has 150 hours of guided meditations allowing you to attain enlightenment. One key feature of the HMJ is that it's a long-term program designed to stay fresh and engaging.

Summary of the HMJ Structure

The HMJ is divided equally into two journeys, comprising 203 meditations each. There is a personal self-development journey and a business one that is entitled the *HappCo Business Journey* ("HBJ"). The two journeys are similar, except for the different persons depicted in some of the series. The personal self-development meditations use correspondingly suitable individual images, such as your significant other, family, neighborhood, club, or place of worship. The business meditations involve images applicable to the workplace, using images of your manager, team, a buddy at work, and company. The HMJ and HBJ are divided into twelve series. Most series are comprised of twenty meditations, and each meditation is about twenty minutes in duration. In addition, there are welcome and exit videos to bookend each series. The HMJ and HBJ invite the meditator to fully experience the prescribed storyline in sequence and numerical order.

Each of the 406 guided meditation sessions is unique to help you maintain interest and focus. Along the way, the tow journeys keep the cognitive mind engaged by consistently offering new relevant insights on how one can become transformed. The transformational process uses your cognitive mind to help break through the illusions that impede your progress. Many of the book's insights and stories draw upon the mini-talks that I give in the HMJ and HBJ.

The HMJ & HBJ Have Coaching

The HMJ gives personal self-development participants a choice between being coached or not. If you choose coaching, you have direct access to my team of Happcoaches and me. With this program, you will receive a personally assigned Happcoach who will track your progress and support you in any way he or she can. For some people, coaching is essential in maintaining a consistent habit. All the wonderful things contained in this book are only available to people who maintain a habit, so if you feel you need a coach, I strongly urge you to sign up for a coaching version of the app. If you sign up with the business version (HBJ), it automatically provides coaching.

The HMJ guides users to enhance their ability to:

- maintain breath awareness (Breathing Into Silence),
- maintain a healthy mind/body dynamic (Mind/Body Integration),
- express loving kindness (Loving Kindness Meditation),
- express compassion (Compassion Series),
- experience abiding joy (Joy on Demand),

- connect with their inner peace (Peace on Demand),
- increase their emotional intelligence (Emotional Intelligence),
- connect with their intuitive wisdom (Wisdom On Demand), and
- create a positive relationship with their inner voices (Discovering Your Magnificence).

Tuning Up Your Spiritual Receiver

The HMJ strategy brings to life the underlying neuronal networks that serve as the spiritual receiver for the Higher Self, which currently exists in a dormant state. Whenever you meditate and quiet your ego-mind, you use your receiver to tune into experiencing your Higher Self. One of the HMJ's key strategies to enlightenment is to allow you the opportunity to experience all of the feelings one has when you connect with your Higher Self. These fundamental feelings are love, compassion, joy, inner peace, and intuitive wisdom. When you learn to experience each of these components simultaneously, you will experience a moment of enlightenment. When you sustain that experience for most of the day, you have attained enlightenment.

For a more specific explanation, let's get back to your meditation session. At the beginning of the first session, where you start on your journey, your ego-mind becomes quieted so that you begin to experience your Higher Self. I like to refer to this experience as entering a spiritual realm or space that holds your Higher Self. As you expand your consciousness, it has an inherent spatial feel to it.

Initially, this spiritual space is a bit blurry, ill-defined, and somewhat disorienting. Being your guide, I show you the way. The objective is to get you oriented, comfortable, and familiar so that you can settle into fully possessing the consciousness of your Higher Self.

Transferring your primary state of consciousness from your ego-mind to your Higher Self when you aren't doing your formal meditation during the day is our ultimate goal. In other words, we want to free you up from the cushion. A successful transfer requires a consistent meditation practice. Each of the twelve-meditation series in the HMJ directly addresses every key component of your Higher Self to become alive and sufficiently charged. Your previously dormant neural networks that comprise your receiver connect to your Higher Self and become fully active. This is the key objective of our journey.

It's as simple as that. The only thing required from you is a commitment to go on this journey. The greatest gift you can give yourself is the intention of living life to the fullest. Then you no longer need to be dominated by your ego-mind and can start living your life from the vantage point of your Higher Self.

Q: Why do I need to practice loving?

Because we are dominated by our ego-minds, which are incapable of loving. This is one of the critical reasons life is such a struggle. Our ego-minds are incapable of experiencing love for two reasons. First, it's not our true self and, second, it's based upon fear. One of the most significant obstacles in expressing love isn't only being overwhelmed by the ego-mind's consciousness but the bad habits we develop and the negative experiences we have had that further impede our ability to love.

The biggest impediment is our lack of love for ourselves. The amount of love we have for ourselves is the critical resource we have to love others. In other words, if we can't love ourselves while we are stuck in the ego-mind, we won't be able to love others. One way to overcome this obstacle is to practice the Loving Kindness Meditation Series. This series allows us to resonate with the love characteristic of our Higher Self. When opening our capacity to love, we can then take the next step: to learn to experience the love for ourselves, and then we begin to cultivate the love for others. This same principle applies to compassion, which we practice during the Compassion Series.

Our Higher Self is based upon love, and the ego-mind's domination of our consciousness is based upon fear. This dissonance is at the heart of so much of our misery and unhappiness. The journey can allow you to seamlessly make the transition from a consciousness of fear to one founded in love. It can make a substantial positive change in your life. It can make the difference between day and night.

Neurons That Fire Together

Every time we arouse each key component of the Higher Self, the associated neuronal networks in the brain and in the heart become stronger. When we keep firing them, new and supportive connections are laid down. A wonderful scientific discovery states, "neurons that fire together, wire together;" which helps describe how the positive effects of meditation work and the value of maintaining a meditation practice.[23] For example, when we do the Loving Kindness Meditation, we activate neurons in our brains and our hearts associated with our sensation of love. As these neurons continue to fire, they stimulate new neuronal growth in the activated areas. This assertion is well-documented in functional MRI studies, which show a size increase in specific areas of the brain associated with a meditation practice.[24] The more we practice, we stimulate additional supportive rewiring in the brain, which creates a greater probability that your Higher Self will become established and experienced throughout the day.

How is the HMJ Different From Other Meditations?

The most significant difference between the HMJ and other programs is the HMJ establishes a comprehensive connection with your Higher Self, allowing you to bring your Higher Self into your daily life. It comes down to this: to consistently experience the Higher Self is to combine the feelings of the five key components simultaneously. While I'm writing this down, I'm breathing in these five components, and boy, it beautifully works every single time! Then you may ask, "Why don't I just do that exercise right now, and I should be fine?" The problem is, for starters, that most people don't love themselves. If you don't love yourself, you won't love others and will struggle to experience any feeling of love. Also, it will be challenging to be compassionate because compassion is love in action.

Being able to invite joy into your life is a subtle skill that requires practice. Being peaceful requires a quieting of the ego-mind and being in the present moment for extended periods. To do that requires practice as well, as you use your breath awareness to stay rooted in the present moment. Finally, being open enough to connect with your intuitive wisdom demands an incredibly high degree of focus. What I described is just a part of the skills you learn when you take the HMJ.

Most other meditation programs help you quiet the mind and experience your Higher Self somewhat, making you feel good and enriched. It also helps with your focus and your equanimity. It also helps you feel peaceful, sleep better, and more centered. These are all wonderful outcomes, but they will most likely not get you to attain enlightenment. Why? Because, as I mentioned before, the most significant challenge is to *fully* embrace your Higher Self so that it becomes fully alive – not just part of it but all of it. In enlightenment, the full force of the Higher Self begins to take over your state of awareness so that your ego-mind becomes your servant, no longer able to dominate.

The most popular meditation app programs, such as Headspace and Calm, do provide meditations that are valuable in improving the quality of one's life; however, these programs don't aim at enlightenment for their users. I refer to their programs as "meditation-lite."

They Aren't True Emotions

In understanding the whole HMJ strategy, the fundamental spiritual "feeling" elements of the Higher Self aren't true emotions. They are experiences that are different from our normal set of emotions. Basically, emotions are the body's response to thoughts.[25] However, when we experience the five key spiritual components, we also feel them in our bodies; they don't originate from thoughts but our spiritual experiences. The experiences we generate during meditation, when we quiet the mind and create moments of no-thought, come from our spirit. Meditation is our portal to our spirit and is why meditation makes us feel so good. We get a good intake of the spirit world, which nourishes our Being and provides us with all the things that make life worth living.

> **Meditation:**
> Take three gentle breaths and feel the sensations in your body.
> So, right now rest comfortably within yourself and breathe naturally. Now concentrate on the region of your heart. And now breathe in and out as if your heart were breathing in and out. Do that a few times and then relax.

Maintaining a Practice

HMJ app is designed to provide the foundation for a life-long practice. This kind of spiritual training is no different from the conditioning of the body. If we keep the mind and body in peak operating mode for life, both practices need to be regularly done. Physical exercise improves our muscle strength and boosts our endurance. Exercise delivers oxygen and nutrients to our tissues and helps our cardiovascular system work more efficiently. And when your heart and lung health improve, you have a greater amount of energy to tackle daily chores. The same is true for the consistent practice of meditation. It keeps our connection with the Higher Self and God vibrant and strong enjoying a greater sense of well-being.

Should We Teach Students to Go on a Journey?

There is a lot of debate about setting up enlightenment as an objective because many students will keep asking, "Have I arrived yet? Am I now enlightened?" Setting enlightenment as a goal to be achieved can make it hard for some students to stay in the present moment and avoid being so goal-oriented is a valid issue. When doing their practice, students are constantly learning to be grounded in the "here and now," not on future events anyway. They understand that the journey isn't about getting somewhere; it's about experiencing each step along the way. If you do that practice, you will get to your destination.

Mindfulness and Meditation

Before we end this chapter, let's clarify the difference between mindfulness and meditation, which are often used interchangeably. Mindfulness is the practice of maintaining a calm, nonjudgmental state of awareness of what is happening to you in the present moment, including your thoughts, emotions, perceptions, feelings, and bodily sensations, while following your breath. On the other hand, meditations are specific techniques for resting the mind and attaining consciousness beyond the ego-mind. Meditation allows us to dive down into the deeper levels of ourselves to experience our Higher Self and, when we want, genuinely connect with God. In its essence, meditation is a spiritual journey.

Mindfulness and meditation do overlap in many ways. When we do a body/scan meditation, we are being in a mindful state as we become aware of the thoughts, sensations, and feelings in our bodies. We also use mindfulness to help us enter a deep state of meditation as we begin each session. It's valuable to allow ourselves to dwell in our "inner body", which requires us to be mindful and is a great way to continue being fully present during the day. So, mindfulness could be considered a subset of meditation. In our ultimate goal of becoming enlightened, being in a mindful state for most of the day is our objective.

> **Meditation:**
> Take three gentle breaths and feel the sensations in your body.
> Right now, rest comfortably within yourself and breathe naturally. Now concentrate on the region of your heart. And now breathe in and out as if your heart were breathing in and out.
> Do that a few times and then relax.

Rediscovering Who We Are

We need to continually step back and see where we are and be mindful because we are lost within our ego-minds. The following story represents the way we go about our lives. Coming from a long history of achievements with billions of people involved, virtually all humans are blinded from reality. We are hiding behind our wall of fear and illusions.

Golden Buddha[26]

In a large temple north of Thailand's ancient capital, Sukotai, there once stood an enormous and ancient clay Buddha. Though not the most handsome or refined work of Thai Buddhist art, it had been cared for over a period of five hundred years and became revered for its sheer longevity. Violent storms, changes of government and invading armies had come and gone, but the Buddha endured. At one point, however, the monks who tended the temple noticed that the statue had begun to crack and would soon be in need of repair and repainting.

After a stretch of particularly hot, dry weather, one of the cracks became so wide that a curious monk took his flashlight and peered inside. What shone back at him was a flash of brilliant gold! Inside this plain old statue, the temple residents discovered one of the largest and most luminous gold images of Buddha ever created in Southeast Asia.

Now uncovered, the golden Buddha draws throngs of devoted pilgrims from all over Thailand. The monks believe that this shining work of art had been covered in plaster and clay to protect it during times of conflict and unrest.

In much the same way, each of us has encountered threatening situations that lead us to cover our innate nobility. Just as the people of Sukotai had forgotten about the golden Buddha, we too have forgotten our essential nature.

We live our lives covered with a protective layer, which is in the form of our ego-minds, rather than coming from our Higher Self. The primary aim of the HMJ is to help us see beneath our armor, crack it open to see the golden glow within our hearts, and bring it out by stepping into our Higher Selves.

What is it All About?

Ram Dass, in his book, *Polishing the Mirror*, describes the process of spiritual awareness.[27] By polishing the mirror of ourselves, the light of our heart and Higher Self shines through.

> *As the veils of illusion begin to become more transparent, as we recognize the limitation of identifying solely with thoughts and experiences, with so-called objective reality, we begin to reflect a purer state of Being. Removing the dust of impurities and attachments from the mirror of our heart-mind allows the light of our spirit to be reflected. As the layers become more transparent, the light shines through us, and we begin to dwell in a less content-laden, ever-clearer state of awareness. Awareness in*

the heart flowers into love, compassion and wisdom. Polishing the mirror, this process of reflecting on ourselves by witnessing and by bringing our external life into harmony with our true Being, resolves when we identify fully with our soul, and these layers of being merge in our spiritual heart. Perhaps then there is a further stage when we cease to experience ourselves as separate beings, when the paradoxical relationship of subject and object merges in oneness. That last step requires something we can only call "grace."

Meditation:
I invite you to take three deep gentle breaths and concentrate on your heart while you feel your heart breathing in and out. Now, see if you can feel a sense of love emanating out of your heart. If you don't, that is totally fine. Be gentle with yourself.

4

Mind/Body Integration

Embracing Your Higher Self

The miracle of the changing seasons is within the breath; your parents and your children are within the breath; your body and your mind are within the breath. The breath is the current connecting body and mind, connecting us with our parents and our children, connecting our body with the outer world's body. It's the current of life. There are nothing but golden fish in this stream. All we need to see them clearly is the lens of awareness.

From Jon Kabat-Zinn[28]

Mentally Scanning Our Bodies

The first series in the *HappCo Meditation Journey* is the Mind/Body Integration series. The purpose of focusing in on your body is to integrate your awareness of your emotions with bodily sensations. Why is this so relevant? When I give a presentation and ask the question, "Where do your emotions reside?" nobody is quite sure, or a few guess by saying, "I think my emotions are in my head." To the surprise of most people, emotions reside in your body. Your emotions are your body's reaction to your thoughts in the form of sensations. This illustrates how few of us connect with our emotions.

To better understand this whole picture, let me clarify the difference between feelings and emotions. Feelings are the action of sensing your emotions. When you have an emotionally charged thought, that thought generates sensations in your body. The process of becoming aware of these sensations is called your feelings. When a person isn't in touch with their feelings, it means they aren't *in touch* with the sensations in their body; they don't have any feelings. It doesn't mean that they don't have emotions; we all have emotions. It means they don't have the self-awareness to *feel* what their emotions are in the form of sensations in the body in the present moment. If unaware of your emotional states, you are disconnected from reality. This is why body scanning exercises are so essential to healthy living.

Reducing Stress in the Body

The main reason our emotions are closely tied to our bodies is for survival. When we are threatened, and fear is generated, our sympathetic nervous system is immediately activated to prepare to either stand for a fight, take flight, or maybe freeze. In addition, even when a particular danger passes, the emotional shock to our bodies can linger for quite some time afterward.[29] And, if we are continually affected by one threatening situation or thought, our bodies stay in a continual state of arousal or stress, which is harmful to our health. And what makes things even worse is that we generally aren't even aware of this continual stress.[30]

This series will teach us the ability to be in touch with our physiological stress, which represents our psychological stress. We will begin to identify sensations and where they reside, physically. Most significantly, we will learn how to relieve our stress through conscious awareness and breathing techniques. The body scan is a simple exercise. But we tend to go into our practice with many expectations about what we want to have happened. These expectations can get in the way of the process itself. Remember that this exercise series isn't about getting rid of thoughts; instead, the purpose is getting at ease with yourself and being at ease with whatever is happening in your mind and body; bringing them together into one sensation and experience.

Scanning Emotional Patterns in the Upper Body

The initial basic series of meditations in this series heightens our whole-body awareness. For our work, it's preferable to do upper-body scans where most of our emotions reside, including the neck, face, and scalp. While scanning the upper body, it's helpful to assign a specific emotion to each sensation. During meditation, we don't try to explore in detail what each sensation means mentally. We stay with the experience and the feelings. We allow our Higher Self to shine its loving light on these sensations so that it can do its work, which is to bring relaxation and peace to the negative sensations; it's all a healing process.

Dr. Zach

Allowing the Higher Self to Do Its Work

One of the key attributes of consciousness is its self-organizing power.[31] It's our spiritual consciousness that runs our body and keeps it functioning. When the body gets injured, the power of our consciousness organizes the body to heal. The same thing is true for our minds. If things aren't functioning well in our minds, our consciousness works on figuring things out. The great power of the body scanning exercise is the process of focusing this healing ability of our consciousness on an area that has been affected by negative thoughts. Allowing the Higher Self to concentrate on a bodily sensation will begin to clear up that negative energy, and the sensation will dissipate and eventually disappear. Since the cause of a lot of illness is due to sensations that reside in the body for long periods of time, it's critical for one's body and mind to resolve these issues as they arise, which is the most powerful tool to address these issues.

It's natural for us to resist focusing on these negative thoughts and sensations, but resistance only causes disquiet because it causes tension. Training the mind involves no longer trying to control thoughts but, instead, stepping back to observe them. With practice, and once you allow yourself to be loving and accepting of how your mind responds, observation will become effortless. Letting the Higher Self calm you down without trying to figure things out is preferable. The wonderful thing is that the Higher Self will help you figure things out without "thinking" about it. The

Higher Self primarily processes stuff without all the thinking chatter; it does it quietly. This is a highly significant discovery.

The cognitive function of the ego-mind isn't the only problem-solving tool we have available to us. The best approach to solving issues is combining the cognitive approach and our intuitive wisdoms to work together.

Clouds in the Sky

One of the processes we do in this series is learning how to relate to our thoughts so that they don't dominate our consciousness. If they dominate our consciousness, we become disconnected from our bodies. Consequently, this isn't an easy skill to learn because we live in a mind-storm consisting of many thousands of thoughts per day. When we find ourselves caught up in a mind-storm, compounded with sensations and emotions, we can learn to respond nonjudgmentally to our thoughts and let them go. A good image for this process is of clouds floating by in a blue sky. The sky is our awareness. The clouds are our thoughts, sensations, moods, emotions, or inner processes. We learn to sit back a bit and watch our inner processes sail by as if we are watching clouds come into view and then moving on. Our mindfulness practice teaches us not to try and stop our thoughts.

Remember, the quantity of our mental activity during our meditation isn't critical; more relevant is the quality of our awareness. As we inevitably float along on our inner stream of thoughts, emotions, and sensations, we become aware that this inner stream absorbs us. We then learn to shift our attention nonjudgmentally back to the breath and the present moment. It isn't so much how many times we get lost in our thoughts that is relevant but noticing that we are and then coming back to observe them is critical. Also, being gentle and loving with yourself when you do this process is helpful.

> **Meditation:**
> I invite you to stop for a moment to take three breaths and observe your thoughts. Then now see if you can just let them float on by.

Q: What If I Can't Let Certain Thoughts Float By?

There will be many times when you experience thoughts that don't float by with the ease of clouds. Instead, you will hold tightly onto some of your thoughts that are emotionally charged. In so doing, your thoughts may have increased; a single thought gives rise to others. Such mental activity is pretty much the same for everyone. We are all accustomed to becoming involved with our thoughts. It's a lifelong tendency to try to control our reactions, to interfere with our ideas or emotions, and to try to fix things.

When you get lost in a chain of emotional thoughts, it's key to return to focusing on your breath and then doing a brief body scan. It's comforting to remember that you have a choice. An airplane may fly into a storm or above it. So, you have the option to fly into higher altitudes above the storm to observe the calming blue sky above. We will cover this topic in greater detail in Chapter 5: Emotional Intelligence.

When our thoughts aren't heavily emotionally charged, it's a lot easier to notice when we get lost in them. We can usually come back gently to our breath. However, if we get pulled into an increasingly large rush of thoughts, or into a sudden mind-storm, where all kinds of mental activity come bursting out, or if the clouds turn dark, it's much harder to be an observer of these thoughts. As we experience the passing by of our thoughts, mind-storms, and intense emotions will come and go. Getting through these episodes requires patience. The most powerful tool is going back to the breath, which is our anchor to the present moment to relax the mind and reduce the turbulence.

Moods – The Water We Swim In

Besides your thoughts, emotions, feelings, and sensations, your moods can last a few minutes to a few hours, days, or a lot longer. Your mood or quality of mind, sometimes called a "happiness set point," can last your whole life. It can be pretty hard to be conscious of it because it's the water you have always swum in – you are so used to it. Often, we get so caught up with what we are doing during the day that, strangely, we lose sight of how we are feeling until the point where our feelings run to extremes. Then we suddenly notice when we feel especially bad or good. In training the mind, there is a benefit in feeling emotions early on. During the body scan series, the perfect opportunity exists to feel your underlying mood, which might be in the background but is affecting your thoughts. What a remarkable discovery because if we learn not to be afraid of how we feel, then we have an opportunity to become happier and less stressed by facing them directly and not turning away from them.

Setting Intentions is a Mental Vessel That Holds Your Practice

When we establish a steady habit of meditating each day, we want to maintain it. We can lose the great treasures we discover through our inner work if we break the habit. One of the most helpful things is creating an intention, in writing, pertaining to your practice. An intention indicates what you want to achieve and is the mental vessel in which you hold your practice. By including other people in your intention gives it meaning, softens you, and opens your heart. It helps to imagine in your mind's eye the reality that we are all connected, and we are one. If you see your practice as a way of helping us heal this earth and save humankind, you can include this thought in your intention.

> **Meditation:**
> Now imagine in your mind's eye the intention you have in reading this book. Hold that thought. Now feel the sensation that comes up in your body. Locate that sensation and then breathe into and out of that sensation for three gentle breaths.

Practice as Routine

Another critical feature in establishing a habit is creating a daily routine for maintaining a lifelong practice. A steady routine energizes our basal ganglia (located at the base of the forebrain), which controls our daily habits. This function of the basal ganglia is only active when our habits are regular and predictable. When we are erratic or unpredictable, the basal ganglia won't play a role at all.[32] Your practice won't be sustainable if it's haphazard or if you try to use your willpower. Willpower becomes fatigued and tires out easily; the force of will won't work.[33] You can't depend upon it during the day. Just hoping that you will think about doing your meditation during the day, and then doing it will not work. It will just not happen over the long term or even the short term. Keeping your basal ganglia stimulated, reinforcing your habit and routine is your ticket to success. When you establish a routine, for even a short period of time, it will begin to reinforce itself, effortlessly, for the long term.

Choosing Optimum Time(s) During the Day

I like to do my first daily meditation as soon as I get up in the morning, right after I wake up. I schedule my wake up sixty minutes earlier than usual because meditation is almost as restorative and restful as sleep itself without taking extra time out of the day. Also, after a good night's sleep, there is little chance that I will fall back asleep. Sitting in a good, upright, meditation posture should assure that you will stay awake.

If you do your meditation right before you go to sleep, it can increase the quality of your sleep so that you may find yourself waking up with a greater sense of restfulness.[34] For those meditators who are serious about reaching enlightenment, I highly recommend you do each meditation session twice a day, first thing in the morning and right before you go to sleep at night.

If you need this, it can be helpful to set a reminder or an alarm to help establish your daily practice. If you are using the app option that includes coaching, you can arrange a one-on-one session with your *HappCoach* or submit a question during the weekly webcast to resolve whatever issues may arise.

Being Kind to Yourself

One of the wonderful things about a good meditation program is learning how to talk kindly to ourselves. This takes practice. Your Higher Self unconditionally loves for you where the ego-mind doesn't. Those critical, undiplomatic voices in the head are mainly modeled after the way your parents criticized you. The ego-mind adopts them to keep you in line, just the way your parents tried to keep you in line. So, a great antidote comes from kindness, forgiveness, and love emanating from the heart when you practice relating to yourself. Remember, however you experience this process, it's all okay. Everyone is on his or her unique path.

We will talk about this in greater detail in Chapter 15.

> **Meditation:**
> Take three gentle breaths. Now simply be in the present moment. Allow your thoughts to come and go and let them do whatever they want to do. Rest, simply relax, and hang out, staying present and aware.

Time, Patience, and the Present Moment

In handling expectations for our practice, a relevant skill to nurture is patience with yourself. You are probably a person who wants to get things done and done right now. Regardless of the many benefits meditations may have in store for you and those you experienced already, please realize that the practice isn't a sprint but a lifelong journey. Don't think of linear time. Meditation involves expanding the present moment so that it can burst out and reveal to you your amazing true nature. When the heart is in full bloom, time seems to standstill.

Even after attaining enlightenment, a meditation practice for the rest of your life is essential. The ego-mind will always be waiting in the shadows. Thus, keeping the spiritual connection open and vibrant is key to lifelong success.

It's such a pleasure to be in touch with the fruitful consequences of our mindfulness practice in our daily life. The practice will begin to fill our lives with meaning, focus, creativity, and happiness.

Since we are on a lifelong journey together, we need to pace ourselves in a way that keeps us focused on the present moment. And, of course, our mindfulness practice teaches us such awareness. It's good to develop a beginner's mind, which refers to a mindset where we approach each moment without expectations, like a child just beginning to explore; the child takes in each present moment with open curiosity.

We must be patient in learning what we are experiencing in the present moment. How do we respond and operate? Over time I will help you to get your so-called "present moment" legs under you. For now, remember that being skilled at being presently aware is like riding a bicycle. It's tough first to get your balance, and things can be shaky. And, even when you learn to get up and ride well, you still need to keep your mind and body in shape to handle all kinds of situations.

> **Meditation:**
> Just breathe into your heart region. Imagine your lifelong meditation practice in a single image. Breathe into that image three times and let it bring you joy.

Conclusion

In summary, by finishing the Mind/Body Integration series, the meditator becomes more connected with their body. We also explored some of the dynamics between our Higher Self and our ego-minds. We stressed the importance of being loving and gentle toward ourselves. We described intentions as the vessels for our practice and the value of including others in them. We covered breath awareness and becoming grounded in the present moment, which provides the foundation for our practice. We reviewed what it means to establish good habits, maintain non-judgmental awareness, permit ourselves to be who we are, and learn to pace ourselves for our lifelong journey together.

Forget your expectations of how you think you might progress. Whatever you end up experiencing is "whatever you are experiencing," and that's fine. Just let it flow. Meditators with high-powered cognitive minds will experience greater challenges than others. But, through practice, these skills can be mastered by everyone.

Dr. Zach

We turn next to the series about emotional intelligence.

5

Emotional Intelligence – Part One

Dr. Zach

*Habits of thinking need not be forever.
One of the most significant findings in
psychology in the last twenty years is that
individuals can choose the way they think.*[35]

*Martin Seligman, Ph.D., the father of
positive psychology*

Emotional Intelligence or EQ has been studied and researched a lot over the past fifteen years. So, precisely what is its significant attribute, and why was it chosen to be the second meditation series for the HMJ? EQ involves the ability to monitor one's feelings and effectively manage one's emotions while recognizing the emotions of others. It also gives us the ability to discriminate among our emotions and guide our thinking and actions. The meditation tools we develop directly relate to emotional intelligence and give us skills in the same general areas.

The Mind/Body Integration series helped us understand and experience the relationship between our emotions and our bodies. We learned that our bodies generate our emotions as they respond to our thoughts and moods. It's so valuable to be able to scan the body to help "feel" our emotions. And what we are experiencing during our body scans is the best indicator of what emotions dominate our consciousness at any given moment. And then, of course, we learned that we need to be in the present moment to be in touch with ourselves. If we are stuck in our ego-minds, we aren't in the present moment; we cannot "feel" how we are doing, and we will become disconnected from ourselves. The Mind/Body Integration series helps get us better connected to ourselves. And finally, we learned that breath awareness is the critical tool for becoming fully present. Because if we aren't in the here and now, we are "nowhere" and incapable of being in touch with ourselves.

It becomes clear that with these newly learned skills, one's ability to increase one's EQ goes up significantly. We will expand on what we have learned in the Mind/Body Integration series to learn more about the STOP and the Expanded STOP method. These tools will not only increase our EQ but will assist us in creating the life we have only dreamed about living. We will break out of our conditioned responses based upon past traumas and develop new responses that work better for us at our jobs and in our personal lives. By navigating the emotional realm, we become sensitive to our emotional states and, concurrently, to those around us. Besides, emotions give richness to life.

Resilience

Another significant attribute of EQ is resilience, which may be compared to a shock absorber. When we are "hit" by a shocking emotional event, resilience softens the impact and enables a quick rebound to return to a positive state. Resilience has two facets, according to the dictionary.[36] It's *the ability to recover from or adjust easily to misfortune or change.* Both recovery and adjustment are involved. Mindfulness will help us with both. We recover more easily from negative stimuli because, thanks to meditation, we get more centered by connecting to our Higher Self and by quieting the ego-mind. Emotional intelligence is related to resilience because, as we can better discriminate among our emotions, we can better manage our thinking and actions and not be caught off-guard as much as before. By having greater awareness, we make better choices on how we respond to shock to be more prepared when it comes.

Scanning the Upper Body: The Basic Skills for the STOP Method

The acronym for the STOP Method stands for: *S*top what you are doing, *T*ake a breath, and *O*bserve your thoughts, sensations, or moods by scanning your upper body and locating the areas of greatest sensation. And then *P*roceed with the day.

To develop the skills for the STOP method, which is a powerful tool to increase one's emotional intelligence, we create intimacy during our meditation with our emotions and related feelings, which strengthens our relationship with the body. We do that through an exercise exploring the emotional/physical landscape of the upper body. Before we do that, we first connect with the breath. After a few breaths, we focus our awareness on our upper body. By scanning the upper body, we sense the tensions and emotional tones, which reside and persist while simultaneously feeling the breath. Then we can create a picture of the emotional/physical landscape. We ask ourselves whether we feel any pain, tightness, discomfort, or maybe comfort or lightness in the upper body. Then we characterize which emotions dominate. If you can distinguish the emotions you feel, then describe them. It's essential not to get into the particulars in great detail. Then, instead of trying to analyze them with your ego-mind, feel them from a slightly removed vantage point, from your Higher Self, by being an observer so that you can experience them.

Our intention is to become aware of our sensations and emotions and, if they are negative, to alleviate them.

> **Meditation:**
> Now take three gentle deep breaths and feel the sensations in your upper body.

The STOP Method During the Day

At the end of the meditation, I advise the meditator to imagine a few moments of stress that regularly occur during the day that might be good times to practice the STOP method. Again, STOP stands for: *S*top what you are doing, *T*ake a breath, and *O*bserve your thoughts, sensations, or moods by scanning your upper body and locating the areas of the most significant sensation. And then *P*roceed with the day.

Dr. Zach

Super Awareness

The STOP method develops a kind of super-awareness. Opening our consciousness, emotions, and feelings, including their interactions with the body, in unforeseen ways. The breath alone isn't only influential in bringing life energy to the body, but it anchors us in the present moment. As time goes on, the present moment will become our predominant focus, though at first, it plays only a minor role. The STOP method combines the power of being present with our life-breath. By focusing our awareness on a specific emotion in an area of the body, we meditate upon it with the Higher Self. This method intends to identify and let go of negative and fear-based emotions that don't serve us. We alleviate them so that they don't persist and become chronic. Or we may learn how to avoid and re-channel certain negative emotions altogether as they occur.

The STOP Method can occur during a relaxing moment or interrupt an incredibly emotional moment that shocks your system. With practice, you can break some of your negative conditioned responses, and you can experience, vividly, the value of this method in helping you get through the day.

By opening a window into the emotional and bodily processes, we learn ways to observe and enhance their positive impact if they are initially positive. However, many of us are constrained and enslaved by negative conditioning. These new skills can reduce the number and intensity of these negative conditionings and lighten our load to experience the present moment with greater energy and enthusiasm. This awareness allows us to change our behavior by helping us make better and more productive choices on how we respond to stimuli. This all starts with awareness. We all want to live happier lives, which are more loving and productive, and when we have choices, that is a godsend.

> **Meditation:**
> I invite you now to practice the STOP method. First, feel your breath and gently rest your awareness on your breath as you breathe naturally. Gently place your awareness on your upper body, scanning to sense the tensions, pains, or emotional tones there, while simultaneously feeling the breath.

Dealing with the Avoidance Response

The STOP Method gives us new skills. Yet, there remain a few hurdles. Naturally, we have developed adaptive patterns to deal with the stresses and strains of life. One such adaptive pattern is avoidance. We avoid things that hurt us and cause us pain – mainly fear. I can't stress enough how damaging emotional avoidance can be to our emotional well-being and the health of our bodies.[37] [38] So much has been written and studied correlating illness with repressed negative emotions. This ability to be aware of negative emotions and avoid fearing experiencing them is a skill one can develop in maintaining a healthy life.

The STOP Method is quite the opposite of the habit of repressing negative emotions. In avoidance, we choose not to work on being consciously aware of our stresses and negative conditioning. With our new skills, we can reduce and process our stress through awareness. By the power of consciousness, we can keep our fear-based energies moving through and out of our bodies. All of us are living with emotional pain, and some with physical pain too. The STOP method helps us stay present and aware rather than go unconscious into the past or future. Remember, there is a simple truth that you will be incapable of feeling and being conscious of your emotions when they arise if you aren't in the present moment.

By developing super-awareness, the STOP method gives us choices. Without this method, our emotions play out in our bodies, and we stay anxious, fearful, or unaware. Then we can't localize our emotions, nor do we have the tools to process them. The natural response is to ignore them. We may drink, take drugs or try to get away from our uncomfortable moods or feelings. Our new awareness means we can process the emotions and move them through and out of our bodies. Thus, they won't pile up or weigh us down. Drinking and drug-taking don't allow us to process any negative energies; the negative stimuli accumulate. Our new tools include quieting the ego-mind, harnessing the power of the breath to keep us in the present moment, and using our super-awareness to stay focused so that we may feel where our emotions play out in our bodies. With our Higher Self, we savor and remain present. What an excellent set of tools!

The Expanded STOP Method –the Next Step

Let me now describe to you what the Expanded STOP Method is all about. The significant difference, as compared with the standard STOP method, is that while you are shining your light of awareness on your emotional/physical landscape in your upper body, you then keep your focus on the most significantly charged area in it. Then you start breathing in and out of that area as if that part of your body were breathing air (or energy) into and out of it. You then do this for a while until the feelings of discomfort there begin to dissipate or disappear.

How do these areas of concern become resolved? Once your Higher Self focuses on something that needs attending, it uses its healing powers to clear it up. For some readers, this may seem a bit unrealistic. Suppose you go back and think about how the body functions in an incredibly sophisticated way just to maintain the body's status quo. The job of unraveling a "negative knot" in your body is like child's play. Remember that consciousness is an organizing force, and its healing power is constantly functioning at a high level. We are just using the capabilities that we already have in a new and unique way. It works!

Breathing Exercise: Golden Light [39]

Meditation:

Let's have some fun with our next breathing exercise, which you can do with your eyes open as you read along. First, focus on your chest. Now, breathe in and out through your heart. Breathe deeply. Now, imagine that a golden mist is filling the air around you, and with every breath, you aren't merely breathing in air, but instead, you're pulling into yourself this golden mist, this lovely golden substance. Let the golden substance pour through and into your entire body, filling you up, whether you imagine it as a liquid or gas in form. And every time you breathe out, breathe out all of your feelings of unworthiness, self-pity, and pain. Let go of your attachment to pain, whether it be physical or psychological. Also, breathe out anger and doubt. Keep breathing in the golden mist and breathing out the things that aren't working for you. Do that for the next three breaths.

Great work!

Predictor of Success

Emotional Intelligence is a predictor of success, both personally and vocationally. [40] [41] [42] We now can recognize the benefits of a calm and clear mind as the foundation for EQ. By training our attention and self-awareness, we can create a calm and clear quality of mind. We now have high-resolution perception into our own cognitive and emotional processes. We observe our inner stream of thoughts and emotions with clarity. This self-observation creates self-knowledge and eventually enables self-mastery, which in turn improves our levels of happiness.

A Good Definition of Happiness

You may have asked why I chose the name of our company HappCo.

Well, the company brand name is short for the "happy community" or "happy company." So, then, what is true happiness? Meaningful happiness isn't merely a pleasurable feeling, nor a fleeting emotion or mood. Instead, deep happiness arises from the ability to quiet the ego-mind, thus allowing the Higher Self and God to shine through you. The brighter the spirit you feel inside you, the happier you will be. We are traveling on a worthwhile journey.

Expectations:
The Chattering Mind

The HMJ guides meditators to go into each session without expectation. Users shouldn't judge their progress because everyone has their style and rhythm. When the ego-mind chatters by saying, "You should be farther along," or by asking, "Is meditation valuable or right for me?" remember that your ego-mind may feel threatened. The ego-mind is accustomed to being a master. During meditation, you are treating the ego-mind merely as a servant by keeping it quiet. Naturally, to maintain its power, the ego-mind will react by trying to undercut your expectations and defuse your excitement about meditation and your discovery of the Higher Self. Remember, the ego-mind tries to keep its status as the master of your consciousness rather than be demoted to servant status. It has a survival mechanism all its own, and it wants you to believe that the ego-mind is your essence and all that you are. When the ego-mind begins chattering, do the expanded STOP method.

Where Does Quiet Come into the Picture?

Meditation makes use of quiet or quiet space as one of the key portals into the Higher Self. Quieting the ego-mind aims to create a state of peace. In this experience of peace, it's the Higher Self that is shining on through. By quieting the ego-mind and being in the moment, we learn to be present, attentive, and loving.

> **Meditation:**
> Let's do something a little different. Right now, with your eyes open, follow your breath, allow your ego-mind to become quiet, and then place your awareness within your heart. Just be with that. Settle upon the ground where the heart can be present and shine. As you do that take three gentle breaths.

Inner Body Discussion

Inner body awareness, as mentioned, is a skill to teach you to stay in the present moment. Eckhart Tolle, the author of *The Power of Now* and *A New Earth,* refers quite a bit to the inner body.

> *In your natural state of connectedness with Being, this deeper reality can be felt every moment as the invisible inner body, the animating presence within you. To "inhabit the body" is to feel the body from within, to feel the life inside the body and thereby come to know that you are beyond the outer form.*[43]

The inner body is the place within us that is an energy field that we can feel. It's a place within us that we sense when we scan our physical/emotional landscape in discovering the areas of physical discomfort or feelings of pleasure and lightness. So, when I write about scanning the emotional/physical landscape, I'm referring to the inner body. Part of our meditation practice is about learning to place our awareness within our inner body so that we keep in touch with the feelings, emotions, or moods that arise as they occur, not only during our meditation but during our everyday living. It's the best place to stay connected with what is going on with yourself internally.

Tolle recommends that we place our awareness into our inner body much of the day. And this is incredibly relevant because we have been brought up thinking we need to place our consciousness within our ego-mind to function properly. We believed that active thought chatter is usual and necessary to function in this world. What if I told you that our Higher Self does have normal thoughts, but it mainly operates without thought chatter? Know that if you experience quiet and a sense of peace, that doesn't mean your Higher Self isn't thinking in the background, subconsciously. It thinks primarily on an intuitive level and does so quietly. A good analogy is that the Higher Self is like a quiet Tesla electric motor compared to the ego-mind, which is like a noisy internal combustion engine. The Higher Self functions mainly within the realm of experiences and feelings.

Tolle also recommends that it's a good idea to dwell a lot within your inner body, so you aren't entirely consumed by the ego-mind's chatter and the extraneous, external goings-on in your life. It's helpful to maintain this balance.

The Pain-Body

Eckhart Tolle has presented in his two books the existence of the *pain-body*. This is a contribution he has made in helping us understand the internal dynamics affecting our inner bodies and our physical/emotional landscapes. Tolle writes:

> *As long as you cannot access the power of the Now, every emotional pain you experience leaves behind a residue of pain that lives on in you. It merges with the pain from the past, which was already there, and becomes lodged in your body. Of course, it includes the pain you suffered as a child, caused by the unconsciousness of the world into which you were born.*

> *This accumulated pain is a negative energy field that occupies your body and mind. If you look at it as an invisible entity in its own right, you are getting quite close to the truth. It's the emotional pain-body. It has two modes of being: dormant and active. A pain-body may be dormant 90 percent of the time; in a deeply unhappy person, though, it may be active 100 percent of the time. Some people live almost entirely through their pain-body. In contrast, others may experience it only in certain situations, such as intimate relationships or situations linked with past loss or abandonment, physical or emotional*

hurt, and so on. Anything can trigger it, particularly if it resonates with a pain pattern from your past. When it's ready to awaken from its dormant stage, even a thought or an innocent remark made by someone close to you can activate it.[44]

The pain-body lives in all of us all the time. As Tolle states, each of us experiences the pain-body differently. Later in his books, he presents a controversial concept that each of our pain-bodies possesses energies from our present lives and includes the collective lives of all humanity, currently and from the past.[45] I know that, for some readers, this can be a turn-off. I want to point out that Tolle's theories on this topic are consistent with Carl Jung's theories of the *collective unconscious* derived from ancestral memory, experiences and is common to all people.[46]

I won't refer to the pain-body again in this book, but I want you to remember the full impact emotional intelligence has on our lives. Also, I want to comment on the importance of the STOP method regarding the pain-body. Tolle mentions that when we aren't in the present moment and mindful, an active pain that isn't fully experienced leaves a "residue." The expanded STOP method, which uses the power of the breath, deals with these negative energies and prevents residues from forming and cleaning up existing residues, regardless of when they were created. We use our awareness to act like a combination mop and vacuum cleaner.

> **Meditation:**
> Let us practice the STOP method again. First, feel your breath and gently rest on your breath as you breathe naturally. Gently place your awareness into your inner body, scanning to sense the tensions, pains, or emotional tones there, while simultaneously feeling the breath.

Conclusion

The meditator that has completed this EQ series will now have meditated over thirteen hours. This is comparable to a four-day retreat that includes three hours of meditation per day! That is a good deal of practice, and much has been experienced and learned so far. A great foundation has been built, and now the meditator is ready in the upcoming series to explore and energize the five key spiritual elements that comprise our Higher Self. In Emotional Intelligence #2, we will return to learning and experiencing more powerful tools to take our EQ to a whole new level. We will be rewiring our internal interpretations that determine how we negatively respond to events in our lives. We will create new ways of responding based on the choices that work for us. It's an exciting series that I know you will love.

Next, we will begin the Breathing into Silence series, a short interlude before starting the Loving Kindness Meditation.

6

Breathing Into Silence

The spirit's so near that you can't see it! But reach for it… don't be a jar, full of water, whose rim is always dry. Don't be the rider who gallops all night and never sees the horse that is beneath him.

Rumi, 13th century Persian poet

Introduction to Breathing Into Silence

This series is a little breather, literally, in our guided meditations. Some people report to me they want more quiet time during the earlier meditation sessions. So, for those who do, these subsequent sessions are filled with a good amount of quiet, and the meditator can spend more time with their breath, to be in a state of just being, using breath awareness as their essential portal or doorway into their Higher Self. It makes sense that we equate silence with the Higher Self, because that experience doesn't include sound. Thus, there is only silence, peace.

I have commented that your minds will wander quite a bit, and you should remember to be gentle with yourself when it does. Our Higher Self is totally patient and holds us in a state of love and compassion. So, if you find yourself being self-critical, realize it's your ego-mind being activated. To quiet it, go back to your breath. This gentle attitude will prepare you well for the upcoming Loving-Kindness Meditations.

119

Golden Mist Breathing Exercise

After the abbreviated body scan, I lead people into doing the golden mist breathing exercise, which we just experienced earlier in this book. I love this exercise because it allows our imagination to transform the "simple" process of breathing. It allows us to take the in-breath, which is usually nondescript, and turn it into a powerful tool. We transform the in-breath into a dynamic phenomenon, whereby the body now feels like it's taking on a golden glow. This helps us feel the incredible energy the body has, innately, and bring it alive in a unique way. And on the out-breath, the imagination also can feel the negative emotions, just flowing out of our bodies on each out-breath, with a resulting sense of relief and lightness.

Dropping into Silence

The second breathing exercise is a little more challenging. We see if letting go of breath awareness while keeping our breathing calm and relaxed results in a deeper connection with the Higher Self. If not, over time, we will work on experiencing being the observer with a greater sense of awareness. Right now, we are just planting seeds.

> **Meditation:**
> Keep your eyes open and start gently riding your breath and staying centered in your breathing for a few breaths. Now drop your breath awareness and stay with the silence while you trust in the openness of your consciousness. Very good!

There will be many more and expanded breathing exercises that we will experience in the future. The quiet time will increase as everyone develops a more remarkable ability to keep their minds focused. It's easy to become frustrated when your ego-mind starts chatting away. I have been diligent about creating a gradual change to the quiet periods as the journey progresses to support as many meditators as possible. Those who are more skilled will become frustrated that there isn't enough quiet time but dealing with the frustration with equanimity is a good exercise for them. Those who are less skilled need a slow increase of quiet time to not get consumed by distracting thoughts. I want to be sure we don't lose anyone along the way.

So, now that we have had this breather, everyone should be fully ready for the Loving Kindness Meditation Series, which is all geared up and ready to go.

7

Loving Kindness Meditation

Love is the life and feeling in the universe. Life without Love Is an empty shell.

Rumi [47]

"Love yourself first and everything else falls in line.
You really have to love yourself to get anything done in this world."

Lucille Ball

I Don't Love Myself?

About five years ago, I signed up for a Tony Robbins four-day event in a large convention hall in the Meadowlands in New Jersey. What a scene! It was a self-help rock concert with Robbins holding court. I got a lot out of the experience. During one of the workshops, I suddenly realized two things in rapid succession: I didn't love myself, and I could not love someone else!

This epiphany shook me to the core. I then stood up from my seat and looked out over the ocean of participants sitting in this gigantic conference hall and realized that probably everyone in the place was swimming in the same sea as I was. They probably didn't love themselves, either. Later I realized that this *is* the state of the human condition. And how could that possibly be true – especially given that the Golden Rule is a core belief at the heart of most major religions and cultures, both ancient and present?

The golden rule states: "Love your neighbor as you love yourself." If people don't love themselves, how are they going to love their neighbors? What is going on? And why is John Lennon's hit song, "All we need is Love," still resonating in our ears and hearts after so long? The song became a worldwide sensation in 1967.

Because of this awareness, every day I include a component of the Loving Kindness Meditation (LKM) in my daily practice. I do this because I want to learn, down into my bones and through my nervous system, that I'm lovable and that I can love. Love is at the core of our Higher Self and, for us to live a happy life, we need to affirm that as often as possible.

The primary function of this practice is to stimulate the part of the receiver to our Higher Self that resonates with loving kindness. The secondary function is to increase our ability to love ourselves and others and be lovable in return! Basic components of LKM have been around for many centuries and adopted in many cultures and religions worldwide. An excellent way to think about the power of love and how pervasive it is is to think about its energy being the predominant feeling of the universe.

What Are the Different Types of Love?

Let's first answer the question, "What is love?" There are three different types of love. The first kind is physiological or sexual love. A second kind is romantic love, through which you make a connection with the ocean of love, inside of us and within another person. This love centers within the context of personal relationships; however, it entails a sense of ownership; that is, the idea that a person is mine and belongs to me. These first two are primarily emotions. The third type of love is our innate or foundational love, experienced from the Higher Self. This is the love Rumi was writing about: "Love is the life and feeling in the universe." Amazingly – are you ready for this? – innate love isn't an emotion. Emotions are fleeting. They come and go, and they react to stimuli. However, innate love is at our core, within our Higher Self. This love is our life energy, which flows constantly.

Now, you still may ask, "Doesn't our innate love come and go?" No, though it may appear that way. It's always there. It's our awareness of this love that comes and goes. We become aware of it when we quiet the ego-mind and experience the present moment within the consciousness of our Higher Self. Since we aren't always in our Higher Self, it seems to be coming and going. Our innate love is our life energy. External circumstances don't influence love, and our true love is defined by the depth and expanse of our spirit, which some people believe is infinite.

The hard reality is that when we are in our ego-mind we can't experience true love. So, when our ego-mind subsides, our Higher Self takes over, and we can begin to live in love. The greatest challenge is that the Higher Self is covered by fear generated by the ego-mind. One of the key purposes of our practice is to cultivate and increase our awareness of the love that permeates our Higher Self. The best meditation for building this awareness of innate love is the Loving Kindness Meditation.

> **Meditation:**
> I invite you to start by taking three deep gentle breaths. Now say silently to yourself:
>
> - *May I be well*
> - *May I be happy*
> - *May I be peaceful*
> - *May I be loved.*

The Benefits of the Loving Kindness Meditation

Throughout the HMJ, we weave in the Loving Kindness Meditation to reprogram negative conditioning, which has been created in our lives by fear, resistance, and confusion. The Loving Kindness Meditation allows us to redirect our attention into our hearts, another critical portal to the Higher Self. Consequently, you will feel that your negative conditioning will weaken its hold on. Within a few days of meditating, you start to feel its effect. You might even feel it sooner. The quality of loving kindness develops as we repeat phrases of the LKM many times over. As I mentioned previously, it's impossible to love someone else unless you have love for yourself. The amount of love you have for yourself determines the brightness of the God of light that shines love out through you to others.

Initially, it can seem challenging to offer love to ourselves. For many, the act can trigger feelings of shame and unworthiness. Yet LKM is a powerful practice, because whatever we don't love in ourselves, we won't accept in another. The inner work comes first.

We project out into the world what resides within us. Years ago, in college, whenever my best friend Danny and I would criticize each other, we would say to each other, "Just hold up that mirror and look at yourself." And the full meaning of that phrase is this: what you are critical about in yourself is what you will be critical of in others. It's one of the most difficult truths for us to face. Whatever burns inside of us is what we project out into the world.

The same thing is true with love. Thanks to our inner work, we open up a pipeline of love for ourselves through the LKM. The overall strategy of the LKM is as follows. First, start with yourself, giving love to yourself while allowing yourself the time to accept your love for yourself. Next, move your self-love outward towards other people. Once this cycle is complete, come back to yourself and do the whole LKM again. I recommended repeating some of the LKM sessions until you start experiencing a good solid feeling of love for yourself before moving on to the next series.

As you are learning, a robust meditation practice isn't about becoming more relaxed. The HMJ is comprehensive: it takes time, the rewards are life-changing, and the practice will allow you to begin to live life to the fullest.

The Science Behind Loving Kindness

There is a lot of scientific evidence proving the benefits of the LKM for cultivating love, our core life energy. Barbara Fredrickson, Ph.D., the Kenan Distinguished Professor of Psychology at the University of North Carolina/Chapel Hill, led research about this topic in the Positive Emotions and Psychophysiology Lab (PEPLab) of UNC. Her book *Love 2.0* establishes that our supreme experience in life is love. Love is a key nutrient that gives us sustenance.[48]

In a rigorous, double-blind study, published in 2008, she clearly showed that the Loving Kindness Meditation had benefits even for newcomers to meditation.[49] Learning to quiet their minds and expand their capacity for love and kindness through the LKM, they transformed themselves from the inside out. They experienced love, engagement, serenity, joy and amusement to a greater degree than before. The LKM enhanced every positive emotion measured. Although the participants typically meditated alone, the greatest boosts in positive emotions came when interacting with others. Their lives spiraled upward. Their kindheartedness, stoked during their meditation practice, warmed their connections with others. Later experiments confirmed that it was these connections that most affected their bodies, making them healthier.

The interaction between the LKM for oneself and with the people in one's life is the winning formula. We will develop more positive relations with our families and friends at home and with our managers, buddies, and coworkers at work (if you are doing the business version -HBJ) because the LKM creates a resonance with the love inside us. This love will spread to every aspect of our lives. Even doing the recordings for the LKM has had an marvelous and positive effect on me when I was in the studio for hours recording the LKM over and over to get it just right. Considering these benefits, I thought my job was one of the best jobs in the world.

Prof. Fredrickson also explains that positive emotions can ignite powerful growth in our lives.[50] They do this first by opening someone up. A person's outlook expands under the influence of positive emotions. Put simply, a widening vision allows a person to see a bigger picture. With this momentarily broadened perspective and more encompassing mindset, we become flexible, attuned to others, creative, and wise. Over time, we also become especially resourceful. Little by little, the mind-expanding moments of positive emotion add up to reshaping our life for the better, making us more knowledgeable, resilient, and socially integrated. Science documents that positive emotions can set off upward spirals and self-sustaining growth trajectories that lift one up to become a better version of oneself.[51] There are powerful positive emotions generated through our LKM as we infuse our consciousness with wishes of well-being, happiness, peace, and love, directed toward ourselves and the important people in our lives. Can you imagine the positive impact this can have in the workplace?

Fredrickson's research has been further developed and tested through additional double-blind studies. She theorizes that positive emotions encourage novel, varied and exploratory thoughts, and actions. Over time, this broadened behavioral repertoire builds skills and resources.[52] For example, curiosity about a landscape leads to valuable navigational knowledge. Pleasant interaction with a stranger grows into a supportive friendship while being creative with our coworkers yields problem-solving skills and outcomes. By contrast, negative emotions prompt narrow and immediate survival-oriented behaviors. For example, the negative feeling of anxiety triggers a specific fight or flight response to secure immediate survival. Positive emotions over time, by contrast, nurture skills and resources to enhance survival by broadened behavior patterns. The LKM helps cultivate pleasant moments of connection with others, which expand awareness. Lasting and beneficial changes accrue in one's life. The improved rapport with your Higher Self can't be overstated.

Positive Psychology

A lot of Prof. Fredrickson's work was stimulated and supported by an innovative domain of study called positive psychology. It was started less than twenty years ago by Martin Seligman, Ph.D., a professor at the University of Pennsylvania. Seligman realized that problems and pathology had almost exclusively preoccupied the field of psychology. Almost nothing was being said about the things that people presently are doing or could learn to do to sustain positive states, such as health, happiness, and well-being. Seligman's early research in positive psychology and his first book on the subject, *Authentic Happiness*, set off a flood of research in the field around the globe to explore ways that people can improve their mental state.[53] And, of course, a lot of research gravitated toward meditation, mindfulness, and quite of few did research on LKM.

> **Meditation:**
> If you again so desire, take three gentle deep breaths. Now briefly scan your inner body to feel what emotions reside there.

Happiness: Degrees of Influence

In support of the results Fredrickson discovered, Christakis and Fowler, of Harvard and Yale, in their book *Connected*, write about their groundbreaking research. They showed that an increase in positive emotions creates a significant chain reaction, enhancing team spirit, creativity, and efficient decision-making for almost everyone around you.[54] These positive emotions can have subtle and dramatic influences on our choices, actions, thoughts, feelings, and even desires. Their research has shown that the spread of influence in social networks obeys what they call the "three degrees of influence" rule.[55]

Everything we do or say tends to ripple through our communities and our companies and affects everyone around us. The people that we directly connect with make up the first degree of influence. Next, the people we directly associate with, who affect others with whom we don't interact, make up the second degree of influence. Then there is the third degree of influence, your indirect circle of people who have their own direct connections. Their study about happiness shows that if you are happy, then there is a 15% greater likelihood that your coworkers will become happier. And the spread of happiness doesn't stop there. The happiness effect at two degrees of separation is 10%. At three degrees of separation, the influence of a person's happiness increases the happiness of his or her third circle by a 6% likelihood![56]

Other researchers have documented that among networks of inventors, innovative ideas seem to be diffused, also, at three degrees of influence. When your company is doing the LKM and generating positive emotions, there is a chain reaction and ripple effect, which reaches in many directions. The overall level of happiness and constructive love feelings improve for everybody. The positive emotions can touch us like waves from distant lands, which wash up upon our shores.

Tight-knit beloved communities provide support systems critical to us in our journey and can help us shift from the ego-mind to the Higher Self. This personal shift in consciousness shows what personal transformation is all about. In looking at the research of Fredrickson and Christakos and Fowler, we learn how positive emotions combined with love, the innate and supreme experience of our lives can improve the quality of our lives immeasurably, and this benefit can continue to spiral outwards over time. Christakos and Fowler's research shows us how these personal benefits and expressions of love and positive emotions will endlessly ripple out, spreading throughout your company's social networks and your communities to create a potentially amazing and supportive environment. The beloved community reverberates the positive emotions that we have projected into it. The transaction is an enzymatic reaction and illustrates that the whole is greater than the sum of the parts. The whole offers strength. Where there is a strong bond of love, your companies and your communities grow more vigorous and more productive. This outcome is exciting, and the LKM is a powerful tool in this process to help make that happen.

Dr. Zach

Stories about the Power of Love

I have included many wonderful stories about the power of love from the HMJ's sessions. The importance of having them in this book is that you get an emotional jolt straight to your heart reading these stories rather than only cognitive input about love.

The first story concerns a high school teacher and portrays a secret power of love, appreciation, and gratitude.

The Teacher and Robert [57]

Some years ago, I heard the story of a high school history teacher who knew this same secret.

On one particularly fidgety and distracted afternoon, she told her class to stop all their academic work. She let her students rest while she wrote on the blackboard a list of the names of everyone in the class. Then she asked them to copy the list. She instructed them to use the rest of the period to write beside each name one thing they liked or admired about that student. At the end of class, she collected the papers.

Weeks later, on another difficult day just before winter break, the teacher again stopped the class. She handed each student a sheet with his or her name on top. On it she had pasted all twenty-six good things the other students had written about that person. They smiled and gasped in pleasure that so many beautiful qualities were noticed about them.

Three years later, this teacher received a call from the mother of one of her former students. Robert had been a cut-up, but also one of her favorites. His mother sadly passed on the terrible news that Robert had been killed in the Persian Gulf War. The teacher attended the funeral, where many of Robert's former friends and high school classmates spoke. Just as the service was ending, Robert's mother approached her. She took out a worn piece of paper, obviously folded and refolded many times, and said, "This was one of the few things in Robert's pocket when the military retrieved his body." It was the paper on which the teacher had so carefully pasted the twenty-six things classmates had admired.

Seeing this, Robert's teacher's eyes filled with tears. As she dried her wet cheeks, another former student standing nearby opened her purse, pulled out her own carefully folded page, and confessed that she always kept it with her. A third ex-student said that his page was framed and hanging in his kitchen; another told how the page had become part of her wedding vows. The perception of goodness invited by this teacher had transformed the hearts of her students in ways she might only have dreamed about.

This story is poignant on many levels. What is fascinating is that the simple exercise of writing down positive things about fellow students, collecting them, and then delivering them to the recipients in writing ended up being one of the most treasured possessions that many of them had in their lives. This story is a great example of the value researchers Fredrickson, Christakos, and Fowler uncovered to improve our schools, communities, and workplaces. Being in the right state of mind, you can probably think of another twenty great ideas just like it.

Are we all so caught up in our struggles that we fail to share how deeply we feel about the important people in our lives? You read about people who grew up and were never told by their parents that they loved them and how this lack created such a big hole in their hearts. And then some were lucky enough to hear finally from their parents on their deathbeds that they did love them. They apologize for having waited so long to tell them. Maybe we are having such a tough time getting through each day that we can't even think that a positive thought might help someone feel better, and we fail to tell others how much we appreciate what they do and who they are. This is what happens when we are in the grip of the ego-mind, which is incapable of loving.

Gratitude

Much has been written and researched about the power of gratitude. I think the list each student received from their classmates was this giant burst of gratitude that kept resonating every time they looked at the long list of positive comments. Robert took it with him everywhere. Gratitude exercises have become so popular because we have such a negative bias in how we live our lives that we can go through a whole day without thinking a single positive thought. By doing gratitude exercises regularly, we can make a positive shift in our overall attitude about life. It's because of its great value that I have added this exercise to the HMJ.

> **Meditation:**
> If you again so desire, take three gentle deep breaths as you briefly scan your inner body to feel what sensations reside there. When you locate them, breathe into those sensations for about five breaths and feel if they dissipate.

Here is another story about the power of the heart. The author is anonymous.

Forgiveness and Reconciliation

He had been a foreign service officer in India for a time, but he had then resigned over a dispute about the US foreign policy; then he started working in DC and Baltimore with young men coming out of gangs, in particular men who had committed homicide. He then told this story.

One of these young men was fourteen years old and lived in a neighborhood where, to protect yourself, you had to get into a gang, and he ended up shooting someone he didn't know to prove himself to his fellow gang members – a sort of initiation, to show he was tough and worthy. These young men were initiating themselves on the streets, which isn't the way it's supposed to happen in this modern world. He was caught and ended up in court and, right after the jury convicted him of manslaughter and before he was taken away from the courtroom in handcuffs, the mother of the boy who was killed, stood up and said to the young boy, "I'm going to kill you!" and then sat back down, and the boy was taken off to jail.

A year later, she went to see him in the juvenile facility and talked to him a little bit. And then she would periodically visit him, and she started leaving him food and then a little bit of money... and then started to make a relationship with him. After four years, when he was ready to get out, when he turned eighteen, she met him at the prison and asked him, "Where are you planning to go?" and he said, "I don't know. I don't have a family and I don't know what I'm going to do."

She said, "I have some space in my house and maybe you can stay there for a while."

"What I'm going to do there?"

"Well, I know a guy who you can do some work with."

So, she set him up and he moved to her house. He began to do this work, and after six months she called him into the living room. She said, "I need to have a talk with you," and he sat down. She said, "You remember that day you were convicted of murdering my son for no good reason?"

"Yes, ma'am."

"Do you remember when I stood up and told you I was going to kill you?"

"Yes, ma'am, I will never forget that."

She said, "Well I did. I didn't want a young man like you, who could go around murdering people, to join a gang, and whatever reason you still are walking around the streets of this earth. I visited you, talked to you and gave you things, and things to read, and brought you into my house, and got you a place to live and a job. I don't have anybody because my son was my only family. I changed you and you aren't that boy anymore, but I don't have a son, so I want to know if you would stay with me and let me adopt you."

Dr. Zach

He said, "Yes, ma'am, I would."
And so, she adopted him. And he
became part of her family.

This incredible story shook me to the core. I was holding my breath, expecting the worst to happen, but it turned out for the best. This story reminds me of the organization I worked with briefly in Israel, The Family Circle, whose members are Jewish and Palestinian families who have lost their family members to violence and civil struggle.[58] They promote forgiveness and love as an alternative to hatred and revenge, teaching people that peace is still possible. Their message is so powerful because if people in such extreme situations can forgive, no one has a valid excuse not to forgive. This grieving mother in our story also shows the power of love and forgiveness. It almost seems if you have love to give and connect to spirit, then the ability to connect to other people to create peace, regardless of the loss or pain endured, has no limits.

Meditation:
Take three gentle breaths and feel the sensations in your body. Think about someone you need to connect with and imagine a bond of affection and if you can make it a bond of love do that. Now think about the next course of action to heal this wound. Now I invite you to take three more gentle breaths.

Letting Loving Kindness Ripple Outwards

At the start of the LKM, we expand our awareness, in a personal way, within our inner consciousness and bodies. Then the LKM involves expanding our awareness, from the individual to the group, continually expanding out to the heavens. Here, we will extend loving kindness, sequentially, to your whole company or your local community, toward all sentient beings on the planet, and finally to the whole universe. Sentient beings are beings that feel, perceive, or experience subjectively.

Concerning the LKM, it's obvious that extending compassion to larger circles beyond ourselves is beneficial. As we have seen, Christakis and Fowler's study shows how our emotions – and specifically, happiness – ripple out to people who are three degrees of separation away from us. How powerful are our feelings and the things we think about in affecting so many people around us? Another famous study showed that we are connected by only six degrees of separation to almost any person in the world.[59] If we double the extent of our happiness impact, as determined from Christakis and Fowler's study, and go from three degrees of separation to six, then our planet starts to act like a small village.

Know Thyself

In ancient Greece, a temple was considered the center of the world, which housed the Oracle of Delphi, where leaders' emissaries throughout the Greek world would come to consult with the oracle before making critical decisions. When the emissaries would enter the temple, they would look up at the phrase inscribed above the doorway to the temple that read: "Know thyself."

The following poem is a little mysterious, but it ties into the importance of knowing yourself. To understand your inner self requires that you drop your barriers of self-doubt, self-hatred, and pain. You are a stranger to yourself until you learn to recognize this stranger as yourself – and then to love yourself without judgment and with full acceptance.

Love After Love[60]

> *The time will come*
> *when, with elation you will greet*
> *yourself arriving*
> *at your own door, in your own mirror*
> *and each will smile at the other's*
> *welcome,*
> *and say, sit here. Eat.*
> *You will love again the stranger who*
> *was your self. Give wine. Give bread. Give*
> *back your heart*
> *to itself, to the stranger who has loved*
> *you*
>
> *all your life, whom you ignored*
> *for another, who knows you by heart.*

> *Take down the love letters from the bookshelf,*
>
> *the photographs, the desperate notes,*
> *peel your own image from the mirror.*
> *Sit. Feast on your life.*
>
> *by Derek Walcott*
> *Collected Poems 1948-1984*

Remember that the foundation of loving others is that you love yourself, even when you seem to be estranged. You do so by connecting with your Higher Self and the infinite love within you. Through the inner work you can get to know yourself better and work through the issues that prevent you from living your own life.

Love is Community

How can love be integrated, personally and in one's family, communities, and companies? The South African archbishop Desmond Tutu explains the interdependence of the person's well-being with the community.[61]

> *In Africa, recognizing our interdependence is called Ubuntu, so when you ask someone, "How are you?" the reply you get is in the plural even when you are speaking to one person. A man would say, "We are well," or "We aren't well." He may*

143

*be well, but his grandmother isn't well, so he
isn't well either.*

This story gives another example of how people's
hearts resonate with others in the same way that the un-
plucked strings of a violin will vibrate with the sounds
of a violin played nearby. A sense of compassion,
which is love in action, is the capacity to understand or
feel what another person is experiencing from the other
person's frame of reference. Compassion involves the
capacity to place oneself in another person's shoes. This
quality is widespread in Africa.

Right after the 9/11 attack, I helped design and
implement a bridge-building workshop to facilitate
connections between the Arab and Jewish communities,
both in the USA and in the Middle East. While there are
many designs for such a workshop, the most effective
exercise is to help people understand the other side's
positions by "walking in the other person's shoes." To
facilitate compassion is the only effective tool for
successful bridge building because compassion is love
with the added motivation to act and reach out to the

other person or persons in need. Rational approaches don't work by themselves.

> **Meditation:**
> If you so desire, take three gentle deep breaths as you briefly scan your inner body to feel what sensations reside there. Now think of someone you have a dispute with and take a moment to walk in their shoes and imagine what they are feeling. Then feel compassion. Take a few more breaths and relax.

Loving Awareness

Sometimes it's nice to be conscious that we are loving awareness at our core. Every day, at 11 am, I remind myself to state out loud, "I'm loving awareness." Our LKM also helps us to bring these qualities into full awareness.

The infinite love that we imagine and experience in our meditation comes from our love essence. The LKM allows us the opportunity to bring out that love at will. This infinite love is real and doesn't just come out of our imagination; your imagination is a conduit through which your true love can emerge. In addition, the desire to give love away and share it reflects the quality of compassion that is also part of our essential being.

A study done a few years ago with 200 college students.[62] The group was divided into two 100-person groups. Each was given $20. One group was told to buy something for themselves, and the other group to buy something for another person. Everyone was tested for their level of happiness at the beginning of the trial to determine a baseline. At the end of the trial, both groups were measured again, and guess what? The group that gave the money as a gift to someone else was significantly happier.

This study has two sides to it. The first is that it's uplifting to see evidence that we become happier when we give to others compared to buying something for ourselves. The sad part of this research is that so much of our society is about buying things for ourselves, expecting that those things will make us happier. The result of this misunderstanding is that there is so much hoarding going on in this world that those who don't have power aren't left with enough to eat or live properly. We have an unfortunate distribution of wealth because of a misunderstanding of what makes us happy.

The following story is also about the heart by Alan Wallace, a leading meditation teacher in the West.[63]

Imagine walking along a sidewalk with your arms full of groceries, and someone roughly bumps into you so that you fall, and your groceries are strewn over the ground. As you rise up from the puddle of broken eggs and tomato juice, you are ready to shout out, "You idiot! What's wrong with you? Are you blind?" But just before you can catch your

breath to speak, you see that the person who
bumped into you is actually blind. He, too, is
sprawled in the spilled groceries, and your
anger vanishes in an instant, to be replaced
by sympathetic concern: "Are you hurt? Can
I help you up?"

In many ways, we are walking through our lives blind, blind to our own reality. We bump into illusions all the time. We deal with people from a place of fear instead of from love. We interact with others not from our hearts but from our chattering mind that isn't grounded in reality. We live behind veils of illusions that meditation can make more transparent so that we eventually can be fully in touch with our Higher Self and become free. When we realize that disharmony and misery come from ignorance and confusion, we can open the door wide to wisdom, compassion, and love within us we can be no longer part of the problem but part of the solution.

> **Meditation:**
> *And say silently to yourself:*
> - *May I be well*
> - *May I be happy*
> - *May I be peaceful*
> - *May I be loved.*
>
> *And now say to yourself, silently, toward someone you care a lot about:*
> - *May you be well*
> - *May you be happy*
> - *May you be peaceful*
> - *May you be loved*

8

From Body to Being

Dr. Zach

*If you want to conquer the anxiety of
life, live in the moment, live in the breath.*

Amit Ray, Indian author and teacher

This series is so named because the HMJ meditators
do a particular practice using the breath as the
portal to the present moment. Of course, the first step is
quieting the ego-mind, then slowly releasing one's
focus away from the body, step by step, by using more
and more subtler sensory images. A fun phrase we use
is "imagine your breath is like a butterfly resting on a
flower petal, in a gentle breeze." Finally, we let go of
these sensations and images by taking a gentle leap
becoming fully present. Once we are in the present
moment, we can experience just "being" independent of
the awareness of the body. That is why we call this
series From Body to Being.

> **Meditation:**
> Just take three gentle breaths while feeling the cool
> air coming into your nose when you inhale and the
> warm air coming out of your nose when you exhale.

Breath Awareness –Dropping Anchor

Breath awareness is the best anchor to the present
moment. Think of anchoring by using the image of a
ship, dropping anchor in a choppy sea. The ship stays
close to the anchoring site, despite the movement of the
wind and water. In the same way, when attention

anchors to a chosen object, it stays close to that object, despite other mental activities. We gain attentional stability. This means bringing gentle attention to your breath. Without good breath awareness, you could not do this exercise.

I want to make clear that, during meditation, you shouldn't expect to be able to quiet the ego-mind fully. The mind will wander; that is true for everyone. The most relevant practice is becoming aware when you are lost in thought, then you are to gently (gently, I can't state this enough, gently, and lovingly) bring your awareness back to your breath. So much flows from this skill. And of course, treat yourself with love and kindness because this begins to establish integrity between how you treat yourself and who you really are.

The Physiology of Breathing

To help us integrate breath awareness into our day, it's a good idea to become fully informed about the physiology of breathing, which Alexander Lowen describes well.[64]

> *The lungs play a passive role in the respiratory process. Their expansion is produced by an enlargement, mostly downward, of the thoracic cavity, and they collapse when that cavity is reduced. Proper breathing involves the muscles of the head, neck, thorax and abdomen. It can be shown that chronic tension, in any part of the body's*

musculature, interferes with the natural respiratory movements. Breathing is a rhythmic activity. Normally a person at rest makes approximately 16 to 17 respiratory incursions a minute. The rate is higher in infants and in states of excitation. It's lower in sleep and in depressed persons. The depth of the respiratory wave is another factor which varies with emotional states. Breathing becomes shallow when we are frightened or anxious. It deepens with relaxation, pleasure, and sleep. But above all, it's the quality of the respiratory movements that determines whether breathing is pleasurable or not.

With each breath, a wave can be seen to ascend and descend through the body. The inspiratory wave begins deep in the abdomen with a backward movement of the pelvis. This allows the belly to expand outward. The wave then moves upward as the rest of the body expands. The head moves very slightly forward, to suck in the air while the nostrils dilate, or the mouth opens. The expiratory wave begins in the upper part of the body and moves downward: The head drops back, the chest and abdomen collapse, and the pelvis rocks forward.

Breathing easily and fully is one of the basic pleasures of being alive. The pleasure is clearly experienced at the end of expiration when the descending wave fills the pelvis with a delicious sensation. Though the rhythm of breathing is pronounced in the pelvic area, it's at the same time experienced by the total body as a feeling of fluidity, softness, lightness, and excitement.

The importance of breathing need hardly be stressed. It provides oxygen for the metabolic processes; literally, it supports the fires of life. But breath as pneuma is also the spirit or soul. We live in an ocean of air, like fish in a body of water. By our breathing, we are attuned to our atmosphere. If we inhibit our breathing, we isolate ourselves from the medium in which we exist. In all Asian and mystic philosophies, the breath holds the secret to the highest bliss. That is why breathing is the dominant factor in the practice of meditation and yoga.

> **Meditation:**
> Just take three gentle breaths while breathing easily and fully. Now take another three breaths as you feel your spirit.

How We Lost Faith

I periodically write about the miracle of life. Reigniting a sense of awe as much as possible is a good thing to stay in touch with how amazing our physical bodies are; this is true for our consciousness. As a people, we have traveled many millennia, absorbed by spiritual and religious influences. Some were well-founded in reality, and a lot weren't. Then the discipline of science came in and threw cold water on traditional beliefs; for instance, by proving that we were no longer at the center of the physical universe, that the earth revolves around the sun, and that there are ten trillion galaxies in the universe. In addition, science defined itself only to include physical things. It ignored the spiritual component of reality, causing a major shift in how we thought about ourselves within the full context of this new insight. We started to feel small and isolated. This feeling of isolation became more acute because we lost a connection with spirit leading to losing faith in ourselves. Spiritual exploration was no longer the major part of the conversation of the day. Thus, spiritual matters became a stepchild during our scientifically dominated era. But, over the past one hundred years, the discovery and establishment of quantum mechanics, this new branch of physics, started turning our whole sense of reality upside down. We started to ask, "What the heck is really going on here?" More and more essential questions about many of the basic scientific assumptions of reality began to emerge. One key area of inquiry is around what role consciousness plays in the full scheme of things. Especially, how does consciousness affect basic physical forms? The most disruptive scientific experiment showed that photons change from a wave to a particle just due to human observation.[65] This is the best clear scientific proof of how conscious awareness alone can make a substantial change to our physical environment. This discovery opened up the need for science to take consciousness more seriously. Coupled with the fMRI studies that showed how meditation changes the brain's structure, science could no longer continue to ignore the 800-pound gorilla in the room – consciousness. This is so relevant to our work because much of our practice is based upon the belief in the power of observation and how it can change the body's energy fields and our consciousness.

Just Breathing is Such a Miracle

In light of this reimagining the world around us, let's further explore the breathing mechanism. Of course, we took breathing for granted before practicing meditation, but let's take another look at breathing to appreciate better when we use breathing as a tool for transformation. We aren't working with a process that isn't so ho-hum; it's beyond belief. As you probably know, when we breathe in air, our red blood cells pull in oxygen (O_2) from the atmosphere and carry that O_2 to our cells. In exchange, we pick up carbon dioxide (CO_2), a waste product of the cell metabolism, and bring that CO_2 to the lungs so that it can be expelled. To maintain a fresh supply of red blood cells (RBCs), the body manufactures two million RBCs every second. Each RBC contains 350 million molecules of hemoglobin, the protein that does the work of gas transfers. Each hemoglobin has 10,000 atoms, and this molecule is a highly complex machine. Now, the number of atoms used each second to keep your RBC count steady is 7×10^{18}. Unbelievably, that number is equal to the number of grains of sand in all of the ocean beaches and deserts in the world! To repeat: the body uses the same number of atoms to maintain our red blood count as the number of grains of sand in all of the ocean beaches and deserts in the world every second! All of this incredible work is done in our bone marrow! It's clear to me that the scope of this biological manufacturing operation is only part chemistry, and the other part is our consciousness at work. Remember, consciousness is the great organizing force in nature, and it so well demonstrates its prowess in keeping us well oxygenated and alive. It's not only a good idea to keep an appreciation of our breathing mechanism but fathom the enormous power of our consciousness. Focusing and working with our consciousness through meditation can do amazing things. The personal benefits of making this a high priority can't be emphasized enough.

The Miracle of the Breath

I'm so fascinated with the hemoglobin molecule because I co-founded and was CEO of a biotech company, Prolong Pharmaceuticals, which uses a modified hemoglobin molecule as its lead product, Sanguinate. In the manufacturing of Sanguinate, hemoglobin is removed from the RBC, and an inert polymer is attached to each hemoglobin molecule to form a tiny RBC. These "nano" RBCs, as I like to call them, treat patients who have disease states that prevent normal large red blood cells from reaching oxygen-starved tissues, thus requiring a physically smaller oxygen transport system. While I was at Prolong, I started doing the calculations, which allowed me to understand the enormous scope of hemoglobin production.

Deepak Chopra and Menos Kafatos, in *You are the Universe*, describe how amazing the hemoglobin molecule is:[66]

> *Hemoglobin is a miracle of construction. Let's imagine walking into the hemoglobin molecule as if entering a vaulted building like a greenhouse with spidery chains of smaller molecules forming the girders and beams. Ribbons of proteins form helixes, functioning like welded bolts. With an eye for pattern, we discern that the protein chains hold a specific shape. There are subunits bonded to the only thing that isn't a protein, the iron atoms – forming rings of proteins encircling the iron. In structural terms there are also specific folds and pockets that need to be in place. A vast space exists so that exactly four iron atoms can pick up four oxygen atoms for transport.*

> *The iron atoms couldn't be inertly encased, the iron had to be charged (as a positive ion) so that it could pick up oxygen atoms. Meanwhile, in the nucleus of the cell, DNA has to remember – and put into motion with precise timing – the whole enterprise*

time and time again. This is a lot to ask of atoms, whose natural behavior is to bond instantaneously to the atom next door and stay that way. Most atoms manage the trick of behaving naturally while at the same time pursuing a creative sideline, namely, life.

This description of hemoglobin and the production process gives us an incredible appreciation for the miracle of life and how consciousness may play the primary role in making it all happen. I write *may play* the primary role, but what else could it be? We refer to life as being driven by a *life force,* but I don't see anything else around that can make life occur but spiritual forces. Our spiritual forces manifest in this world in the form of consciousness. I only see our consciousness running our bodies. I'm implying that our consciousness provides our organizing self-awareness and navigational capabilities to run the body.

Meditation:
Just take those three gentle breaths while feeling the sensations in your body. Now take another few breaths as you feel the miracle of the body. Feel its incredible quiet energy.

Becoming Fully Present

Let's step back to get a fuller perspective on how to become fully present. How can we get there more often and consistently so that this state dominates our consciousness? One thing is clear; it requires practice. It also is a skill that first needs to be learned. A key part of that skill is learning to put our ego-mind at rest which constantly puts us into the past, regretting, and into the future, worrying. Breath awareness is key to doing that. Learning to draw upon the breath all through the day as a habit can be transformative.

The breathing meditation settles us into a state of being, which is calm and peaceful. Our ability to observe our thoughts is the ability to be within the Higher Self's consciousness as a witness. Our observation comes from our Higher Self. And the inner peace we experience isn't just a quieting of the ego-mind, but comes from feeling our inner peace, which is one of the core qualities of the Higher Self.

Our Spiritual Receiver

The great thing is that our neural networks that comprise our spiritual receiver don't need to be created from scratch, it only needs to be discovered and brought to life because it's already in us. Through practice, we fire up pathways that connect with our Higher Self and lay the foundation for enlightenment.

Here is an interesting discussion about our intrinsic nature from Dan Goleman's and Richard Davidson's book, *Altered Traits*:[67]

The yogis who came to Richie's lab
practiced in a Tibetan tradition that proffers

159

a view... that we all have Buddha-nature, but we simply fail to recognize it. In this view, the nub of practice becomes recognizing intrinsic qualities, what's already present, rather than the development of any new inner skill. From this perspective, the remarkable neural and biological findings among the yogis are signs not so much of skill development but rather of this quality of recognition.

Are altered traits add-ons to our nature, or uncovered aspects that were there all along? At this stage in the development of contemplative science it's difficult to weigh in on either side of this debate. There is, however, an increasingly robust corpus of scientific findings showing, for example, that if an infant watches puppets who engage in an altruistic, warmhearted encounter, or ones who are selfish and aggressive, when given the choice of a puppet to reach for, almost all infants choose one of the friendly ones.

This natural tendency continues through the toddler years. These findings are consistent with the view of preexisting virtues like an intrinsic basic goodness and invite the possibility that training in loving-kindness and compassion involve recognizing early on a core quality that is present and strengthening it. In this sense, meditators may not be developing a new skill but rather nurturing a basic competence, in much the same way that language is developed. Whether the whole range of qualities said to be cultivated by different meditation practices is best viewed in this way or more as skill development will be decided by future scientific work. We simply entertain the idea that at least some aspects of meditation practice may be less like learning a new skill, and more akin to recognizing a basic propensity there from the start.

In this passage, Goleman and Davidson state that there is a good scientific basis for an existing neuronal blueprint for behavior referred to as "Buddha-nature." They suggest that we don't need to learn this behavior; we may just need to recognize something "already present." I take this concept a step beyond this particular discussion by believing that this Buddha-nature blueprint is a receiver to the spiritual realm, not a brain-centered phenomenon.

> **Meditation:**
> Take those three gentle breaths and feel a sense of awe concerning what your body has to offer you. Then feel grateful.

The Power of the Focused Mind

Meditation practices develop a more focused mind which is underappreciated. In his book, *The*

Attention Revolution, Unlocking the Power of the Focused Mind, Alan Wallace, Ph.D., describes the benefits of attention and the lasting benefits of a focused mind.[68] The benefits improve a person's character in moral terms, promote creativity and genius in one's work, and yield healing by tapping the resources of the mind.

Attention also has a profound impact on character and ethical behavior. [William] James, [father of modern psychology], felt that the capacity to voluntarily bring back a wandering attention, over and over again, is the very root of judgment, character, and will. Christian contemplatives have known for centuries that a wandering mind easily falls into temptation, leading to sin. And Buddhists have recognized that a mind prone to distraction easily succumbs to a myriad of mental afflictions, leading to all kinds of harmful behaviors. If we can direct our attention away from negative temptations, we stand a good chance of overcoming them.

James also asserted that geniuses of all kinds excel in their capacity for sustained voluntary attention. Just think of the greatest musicians, mathematicians, scientists, and philosophers throughout history – all of them, it seems, have had an extraordinary capacity to focus their attention with a high degree of clarity for long periods. A mind settled in such a state of alert equilibrium is fertile ground for the emergence of all kinds of original associations and insights. Might "genius" be a potential we all share – each of us with our unique capacity for creativity, requiring only the power of sustained attention to unlock it? A focused mind can help bring the creative spark to the surface of consciousness. On the other hand, the mind constantly is caught up in one distraction after another, maybe forever removed from its creative potential. If we were to enhance our faculty of attention, our lives would improve dramatically.

Wallace goes onto describe the healing potency of this practice:[69]

As long as our minds oscillate compulsively between agitation and dullness, wavering from one attentional imbalance to another, we may never discover the depths of human consciousness. Can the mind be irreversibly freed from its emotional afflictions, such as craving, hostility, depression, envy, and pride? Are there limits to our love and compassion? Is awareness finite and immutable? We know that the mind has powers of healing, which are sometimes attributed to the "placebo effect," and that it can make us ill as well. What other powers lie dormant within human consciousness, and how can they be tapped? Contemplatives have posed these questions throughout history, and focused attention has been a crucial tool in exploring them.

Wallace's comments are incredibly significant, especially for this series. This series of meditations require an unusually high degree of focus and concentration. All of the HMJ sessions require focus, but this series calls for a refined concentration in subtle ways to establish a moment of total stillness – withdrawn from physical sensations. Wallace describes the benefits of staying focused on the things one holds most dear.

This book was made possible because I was able to stay focused to write a coherent book and finish it. So many people desperately want to write a book but cannot stay focused enough to start it or, if they do start, finish it. Most dreams are made possible solely through the ability to stay focused. It is kind of scary to think about how critical it is. We refer to the importance of being focused but rarely do we fully appreciate its incredible value. Focus and concentration are essential to meditation.[70] One's attention and memory can improve markedly after just a few weeks of practice.

While these benefits may emerge even with a remarkably modest investment in practice, they are likely fragile. A regular and sustained near-daily practice is required to maintain these benefits.

How Are You Doing? The Happiness Set Point

It is always a good idea to get a sense of how well you are doing in your practice. A good measure is your happiness set point, which indicates how happy you are overall, and it had been assumed that this set point didn't change over time.[71] Things didn't look good for us, according to this assumption. We were told that we were stuck with the hand we were dealt. However, positive psychology research has found three determining factors of our happiness set point: 1. genetics (50%), 2. determined by our actions, our attitude of optimism, and the way we handle situations (40%), and 3. our current life circumstances (10%).[72]

Two things jump out from this research. The first is that our current circumstances play a small role in determining our happiness set point. The second thing is that our attitude and how we handle situations are four times greater than our current situation. In our meditation practice, we learn to be more in the present moment and awake and not let our lives run on autopilot. If we stay fully aware, our lives' full range of choices is made available to us. Thus, we can continue to improve our lives for the better. These tools allow us to tap into our Higher Self, which gives us the power and freedom to change our life circumstances. We are finally capable of making choices that help us to become happier and healthier. In turn, our happiness set point becomes improved. One fundamental choice that we make daily is to practice our meditation.

I was able to increase my happiness set point through meditation significantly. A few years ago, I built the first positive psychology app, which included a chat room, to help build a heart-based community for support. This app was geared to the consumer marketplace with recommended positive psychology activities, including meditation. I did the exercises, such as keeping a gratitude journal, tracking my positive and negative thoughts, and monitoring healthy daily habits of my choosing. I took the app's happiness test every six weeks, while interacting with the other participants.

Although the app didn't succeed in generating a sustained community, nor did it become a successful business venture, it did help me improve my happiness set point. Though people would always tell me that I was a positive, happy person, I still had a deep feeling of unease. After that year of working with the app, my unease diminished in strength, and consequently my happiness set point grew to a more favorable level. I've maintained those improvements now over the past few years, primarily helped by my meditation practice.

The HMJ and the Gratitude Exercise

To assist in increasing the happiness set point for the HMJ users, I decided to take the gratitude feature I had included in the positive psychology app and inserted it into the HMJ at the conclusion of each meditation. This provides an opportunity to record three things for which you are most grateful. Gratitude exercises can have a significant impact on your happiness set point, and the research proves it.[73]

Breath Awareness During Your Day

As a meditator, one should always look for good ways to integrate breath awareness into your daily activities. Some good suggestions are when you wait for an elevator, or at the copy machine, or for a website to load. Immediately bring your awareness to your breath until your wait is over. Before you developed this habit of breath awareness, waiting was a drag, and, of course, you immediately pulled out your phone to bide your time. Now you can use these times to become aware of your breath and quiet the ego-mind, thus bringing forth your Higher Self at will. Convert wasted time during the day into invaluable time. How sweet!

Making Plans While Staying in the Present Moment

Providing the space to allow our Higher Self into our everyday living requires us to be in the present moment because living life in the past and future isn't truly living in a state of reality. But in reality, we need to plan ahead by looking to the future and analyzing our past to learn from it. Let's consider a reasonable question, "How can we plan out our future events while we practice staying in the present moment?" Tolle writes an elegant discourse on the subject:[74]

Dr. Zach

Learn to use time in the practical aspects of your life – we may call this "clock time" – but immediately return to present-moment awareness when those practical matters are dealt with. In this way, there will be no buildup of "psychological time," which is identification with the past and continuous compulsive projection into the future.

Clock time isn't just making an appointment or planning a trip. It includes learning from the past so that we don't repeat the same mistakes over and over. We are setting goals and working toward them. Predicting the future using patterns and laws, physical, mathematical, and so on, learned from the past and take appropriate action based on our predictions.

But even here, within the sphere of practical living, where we can't do without reference to past and future, the present moment remains the essential factor: Any lesson from the past becomes relevant and is applied now. Any planning as well as working toward achieving a particular goal is done now.

The enlightened person's main focus is always the Now, but they are still peripherally aware of time. In other words, they continue to use clock time but are free of psychological time.

Be alert as you practice this so that you don't unwittingly transform clock time into psychological time. For example, if you made a mistake in the past and learn from it now, you are using clock time. On the other hand, if you dwell on it mentally, and self-criticism, remorse, or guilt come up, you are then directing the mistake into "me" and "mine": You make it part of your sense of self, and it has become psychological time, which is always linked to a false sense of identity. Unforgiveness necessarily implies a heavy burden of psychological time.

If you set yourself a goal and work toward it, you are using clock time. You want to be aware of where you want to go, but simultaneously, you honor and give your fullest attention to the step you are now taking. If you become excessively focused on the goal, perhaps because you seek happiness, fulfillment, or a more complete sense of self in it, the Now is no longer being honored. It becomes reduced to a mere stepping stone to the future, with no intrinsic value. Clock time then turns into psychological time. Your life's journey is no longer an adventure, just an obsessive need to arrive, to attain, to "make it." You no longer

see or smell the flowers by the wayside either,
nor are you aware of the beauty and the
miracle of life that unfolds all around you
when you are present in the Now.

Tolle writes about being dependent upon staying within the present moment, which requires embracing your Higher Self. As soon as you get recaptured by your ego-mind, you will immediately get stuck back into the past/future dilemma. There will be no clock time because you won't be in the present moment. The more intensely and consistently you do your meditation and use the power of the breath, the more able you will be to stay fully in the now.

Wisdom 2.0: Mindfulness in America – Staying Present

At a recent *Wisdom 2.0 – Mindfulness in America* conference in New York City, an afternoon dedicated to the challenges new technologies place on us in staying in the present moment.

The founder of Nest, Tony Fadell, spoke with Anderson Cooper, the CNN journalist, about the importance of present awareness given the distractions of technology. Fadell is the man who oversaw the creation of the iPad and the first three versions of the iPhone. Fadell advises us to find the discipline to keep technology in its place and live in the here and now. He mentioned that it was helpful for millennials to do meditation to counteract too much screen time. Young people spend minimal time in the presence of life. Instead of looking into the eyes of their friends, they are captivated by the glow of their screens. I realize how much my phone is invading my space. I even take my phone into the bathroom with me. Arianna Huffington also spoke, saying that she leaves her phone outside her bedroom to get sufficient and uninterrupted sleep. Technology can make a great contribution and can also have unexpected consequences. The importance of being aware and making the right choices is the trick to success.

Exit Exercise for the Breathing Series

I have added a new component to the traditional exit routine in our meditations by keeping our eyes open. This exit exercise is designed to provide a smoother transition, so that you may transfer your breathing and self-awareness skills, developed during your meditation practice (with eyes closed), to the demands of the rest of the day when your eyes are open. That way, your skills won't be dependent on having your eyes closed. This exit "ramp," allows a gradual transition. Because the transition isn't easy, I advise you to be patient with yourself. Like a gentle off-ramp movement, this exit exercise combines components of our meditation, including awareness of the breath, body, and emotions. This helps to integrate your mindful state into your everyday waking life as you learn to focus on the present moment by anchoring your awareness on the breath and the inner body. Our ability to call upon the breath as our anchor at any time is a potent tool. At some point, it is key to look at our life as a meditation.

Meditation:
Take three gentle breaths and concentrate solely on your breath.
Then think of one thing to be grateful for. Now breathe into and out of that thought with three breaths.

Conclusion

Congratulations. We focused upon a broad spectrum of topics in this chapter. We explored how miraculous our bodies are, how our consciousness may be very much involved in how our bodies function, and ways we can become more fully present. We covered the primary practice for the Body to Being series where we learn how to experience a pure observer mindset independent of any feelings, sensations, thoughts, or moods. We find ourselves in a state of just being.

You aren't a drop in the ocean. You are the entire ocean in a drop.

Rumi

9

Compassion
Series

Dr. Zach

Our task must be to free ourselves by widening our circle of compassion to embrace all living creatures and the whole of nature and its beauty.[75]

Albert Einstein

To inspire us, as we move into the topic of compassion, I also begin this chapter with a reflection by Thomas Merton, Trappist monk, and Christian Theologian.[76]

Then it was as if I suddenly saw the secret beauty of their hearts, the depths of their hearts where neither sin nor desire nor self-knowledge can reach, the core of their reality. If only they could all see themselves as they really are. If only we could see each other that way all the time. There would be no more war, no more hatred, no more cruelty, no more greed.

What a vision! Merton expresses a view as to the beauty of reality, and human beings, at their core. We may also attain a perception of this beauty, which can relieve the world of its ills. I share this vision and believe that our spiritual practices may lead us there. That is a possibility, a real one.

As we move into the topic of compassion, it's helpful to remember that love is the basic vibration of the universe. Love is like an energy wave upon which we surf in life. Our ego-mind guards us so we don't give everything away because our Higher Self tends to give things away. Currently, the ego-mind asserts control over us and our complex world. Through compassion, we overcome the constraints of our ego-mind. Our freedom grows when we actively help others and our ecosystem (including the critters and the environment) by coming from love. And, of course, it takes practice to open up and widen our relevant neuronal pathways.

Definitions

Let's first review some definitions of compassion and empathy, which need some clarification because these two words are mistakenly used interchangeably. Acknowledge that definitions of these terms do vary according to psychologists and other professionals.[77] Research supports the following definitions and is pertinent to our meditation practice.

Empathy is a skill and capacity to understand or feel what another person is experiencing from within the other person's frame of reference. Empathy involves walking in another's shoes to feel the suffering or joy of another without necessarily doing anything to help or to support that person. There is no action component to empathy. When you feel compassion, you are also in the other person's shoes and feel the suffering of another, and you have a desire to take action to relieve another's suffering. Sympathy is to feel sorrow for the hardships of others. Finally, pity is a feeling of discomfort at the distress of others and often has paternalistic or condescending overtones.

Big Difference Between Empathy and Compassion

Because empathy can cause a person to take on the negative feelings of others, researchers distinguish compassion and empathy in the following way described in the book by Stephen Trzeciak, MD, entitled *Compassionomics: The Revolutionary Scientific Evidence that Caring Makes a Difference*:

> *Taking action to relieve another's suffering is at the very heart of being compassionate and bringing rewards that can overcome the distress of empathy.*[78]

> *Most scientists define compassion as the emotional response to another's pain or suffering, involving an authentic desire to help. It is different from empathy, which feeling and understanding (that is, detecting and mirroring another's emotions and experiencing their feelings) because compassion also involves taking action. Feeling empathy is a necessary precursor (or prerequisite) to motivate acts of compassion, so the terms are related, yet they are also distinct.*[79]

> **Meditation:**
> Let us open up our hearts to the compassion within us
> right now. Experience this powerful part of our
> Higher Self. And just send out some compassionate
> energy to other people who surround you most days.
> In order to exhibit compassion, all you have to do is
> offer some of your very best loving kindness,
> understanding and generosity. Let's do that by taking
> three gentle deep breaths.

The Blessings of Being Connected

The following story is about a boy from Kenya
who, as Archbishop Desmond Tutu mentioned, had a
strong sense of Ubuntu, a strong feeling of
interconnectedness with your family and the
community. This boy's compassion went beyond the
bounds of what his stepmother felt was right.

The Compassionate Young Boy [80]

*Once upon a time, in a small village in
Kenya, there lived a young boy with his
stepfamily. Due to the scarcity of water in the
village, the young boy awoke early every
morning, carried his pot and headed for the
stream with the aim of fetching water for
himself and his stepfamily. Sadly for him, he
alone had this task as a routine every
morning and evening to fetch water from a
distant stream, while his step siblings were*

given other more lenient tasks or even none. Yet, the young boy bore no grudge against his stepfamily, loved them and carried out his task, diligently. On his way back from the stream, he met an old man resting under a tree who begged for water to quench his thirst and he gave water to the old man. He met an elderly woman who begged for water and he gave water to the woman.

This happens almost every time as he comes back from the stream; meeting people who beg for thirst, yet he gives water to them despite his stepmother's torturing him for fetching half-filled pots that wouldn't be enough for the family. One day, he couldn't bear the torture from his step mum, so he swore never to give anyone water, but on his way back, he met a strange-looking man who begged him for water. The strange man lay by the roadside with an injury. The young boy remembered his vow – never to give anyone water – but contemplated for a moment and then gave the strange man some water.

When he got home, his step mum noticed the half-filled pots, and again pounced on him – this time with more cruelty. As she was beating this young boy, there was a knock on the door. It was the wounded strange man – a mail deliverer. Apparently, he came from the town with a letter for the

young boy. A letter contained a scholarship
with an additional cash gift for the young boy
and the messenger would have died on the
way if not for the boy's help.

They say there is love in sharing and Mahatma Gandhi said, "Where there is love there is life." Your everyday good deeds are never in vain, for they shall return to you even when you're not expecting it. Just like the young boy, who was filled with love and compassion and met his blessings at an unexpected hour, you shall meet your blessings for your good deeds of love and compassion as well.

No Good Deed Goes Unpunished

> **Meditation:**
> If again you so desire, take three gentle deep breaths as you briefly scan your inner body. Take what sensations you felt when you read that the boy received the scholarship. Breathe through those sensations in your body and then relax.

I must comment on the popular phrase, "No good deed goes unpunished." I was so shocked when hearing this phrase repeatedly, as if to communicate that it's a bad idea to do good deeds and be compassionate. I first thought, "Has our society gone mad?" Don't ask. So, let's try to understand this phrase and why people are quoting it before moving on. The phrase attributed to

Oscar Wilde, the playwright, or Claire Booth Luce, the author and politician.

The phrase really means that some good deeds aren't well accepted. They sometimes cause the recipient to develop expectations for more help and benefits. The idea is that, in the end, the recipient may not want what you are offering them, or they may feel that they deserve something else (that in fact, they may not deserve). These expectations may lead to a lot of discomforts. Also, when people don't want your help and rebuff your efforts, this may hurt your feelings. In this case, too, you are being punished for trying to help. Look, all of these things are true. When we live in a world where love is having a hard time being expressed and accepted, the phrase has relevance. However, if this idea presents itself as an absolute, I need to call it out. It should read, "Sometimes, you can feel punished for doing good deeds."

Compassion Meditation: Receiving Love

The compassion meditations involve, first, connecting with a loved one. Then you receive compassion and loving kindness back from this loved one. From this foundation of deep love and compassion, you learn to be kind, loving, and compassionate to yourself. This is important because almost all of us are tough and impatient with ourselves. Interestingly, we have a default mode when we aren't engaged in any pressing cognitive activity. We fall into ruminating upon *the I* and *the me*. During this downtime, we may start thinking about the things we need to do, but we also rotate through a cycle of self-judgments, whether they be judging ourselves, our relationships, or our Facebook page. To offset this harsh self-orientation, we can develop new neural wiring and a spirit of gentleness with ourselves.

Self-compassion is the foundation for compassion toward others. The significant thing to be aware of is the presence of the ego-mind. When we are brutal to ourselves, we are in our ego-mind. And when we find ourselves being loving and compassionate towards ourselves, we are in our Higher Self. It isn't in our true nature to be cruel to ourselves or to others. This is the main differentiator between the two minds and is a good fact to keeping track of.

In our compassion practice, we reinforce pathways that allow our Higher Self to break through into our conscious awareness; in turn, we diminish the neural pathways and brain centers that contain a preponderance of painful experiences that have made us fearful of others. Others have hurt us because they were out of touch with their own Higher Self. We also respond while being out of touch with our conditioned responses. So, our history is filled with ongoing pain and suffering. The beauty is that we can break through the grief and pain by honoring our compassionate intentions and become more fully present while bringing to life our Higher Self.

Dr. Zach

Joseph Campbell on Compassion

Let's turn now to consider some thoughts on compassion offered by Joseph Campbell. Campbell was a leading expert in comparative religions, mythology, art, images, stories, and dreams. He dealt with universal structures by which the human species touches the deeper meaning of life. Campbell had amazing insights, although this passage isn't easy to understand right off.

> he key to the Grail or a difficult quest
> is compassion, "suffering with," feeling
> another's sorrow as if it were your own. The
> one who finds the dynamo of compassion is
> the one who has found the Grail. The
> principle of compassion is that which
> converts disillusionment into a participatory
> companionship. [81]

Campbell states, "The one who finds the dynamo of compassion is the one who finds the Grail." This means the hero or heroine is the one who filled with compassion. Compassion offers a sense of direction and purpose so that we may achieve our goals. Thus, becoming compassionate is a key part of becoming the hero or heroine in our personal stories. Campbell says, "The principle of compassion is that which converts disillusionment into a participatory companionship." I interpret that to mean when we are solely focusing upon ourselves and not on the pains of others; we experience life as being devoid of meaning. However, by finally choosing to reach out and connect with others, we essentially acknowledge that our essence connects to the essence of others through compassion. Thus, the pain of life fuels loving companionships rather than isolation and hope rather than disillusionment.

This compassion, and participatory companionship, is at the core of our meditation practice through our compassion exercises. We set an intention for our practice that supports compassion. Intention is the vessel that holds our meditation practice. Thus, what helps give our meditation meaning is to include others in our intention.

We have dealt with compassion so far by exploring the interdependence of self and others. Compassion works similarly to love. To experience true love with others, we need to clear away any misgivings about being able to love ourselves. Thus, to be fully compassionate with others, we need first to be compassionate with ourselves. In this series, we are creating rewiring through our openness to compassion. Since we have been firing neurons associated with compassion, we have laid down a solid foundation. We can then expand our compassion toward people who link to us in love. We can even be compassionate toward those with whom we have some major issues or where hurt, pain, and anger have prevented love and compassion from existing.

Overcoming Hatred

I learned about compassion from my experiences in the Middle East, conducting peacemaking and bridge-building workshops between the Israelis and Palestinians. The organization, the Family Circle, promotes forgiveness as an alternative to hatred and revenge. Such work reminds us that compassion and love are the driving forces for peace and the best means to heal our wounds. If people who have lost loved ones to violence can forgive, others can do the same in much less painful circumstances. Compassion means "to love together with" or, in other words, *true love in action,* regardless of the circumstances.

Heart-based Communities

When I started to write my autobiography, I was able to see my continual focus throughout my life on building heart-based communities. I believed that such work would be an essential springboard necessary to allow humanity to leap to the next phase of its evolution. The following poignant short story is such a great example of how a heart-based community can function.[82]

> *In arid landscapes during ancient times, grapes were rare, a succulent delicacy grown in distant regions. Yet one day, records from the second century AD tell us, someone brought just such a treat all the way to the desert abode of Macarius, a Christian hermit. But Macarius didn't eat the grapes; instead he gave them to another hermit nearby who was feeble and who seemed in greater need of the treat. And that hermit,*

though grateful for Macarius's kindness,
thought of yet another among them who
would benefit from eating the grapes, and
passed them on to that monk. So, it went
through the entire hermit community until the
grapes came around again to Macarius.

In this desert community, everyone was taken care of by the whole community so that love and compassion were allowed to flourish. There was no self-centered concern for any individual's well-being because the community would always look out for you.

> **Meditation:**
> If again you so desire, take three gentle deep breaths. Then imagine you are living in a tight-knit loving community. Then briefly scan your inner body to feel what emotions come up for you.

Trading in Empathy for Compassion

Previously, we defined the differences between empathy and compassion. The critical difference is that compassion stimulates action. However, there are other differences. It's fascinating that empathy can sometimes negatively affect and impact us. When we experience empathy, we feel the pain of others as our own; thus, we are in pain and want to avoid it.

In contrast, when we feel compassion, even in the same situation, we generate positive feelings, which motivate us to take action. In the workplace, a coworker close to us may be struggling. If we only experience empathy, a negative response may be triggered, directing us to ignore or turn away from this person, who may desperately need our help and support. However, having compassion is about positively responding to our coworker. We will be motivated to help them out to find solutions to their problems.

Compassion does include empathy, but, most significantly, love is its key component. It's love that is the key motivator that nudges us to take action.

When the sunshine of loving kindness meets the tears of suffering, the rainbow of compassion arises.[83]

A meditation teacher from Myanmar

Compassion supports us to take action when we see the need for it. The same neural circuitry is activated as that generated by parents who express love for their child.[84] We are stimulating the deepest caring centers. This is why holding people around us in our hearts is so impactful. People feel the love and respond to it. Barbara Fredrickson's theories confirm this point. When love nurtures, we reach out to others with love. Those loving gestures increase the love and compassion that we feel around us. In turn, love comes back to us with positive responses. Our mindful community is a realistic and achievable goal because of this positive self-reinforcing circle of love and compassion.

Embracing Suffering

Most of us shut ourselves off from suffering because it's painful. For me, living in a large city, this is so true. I see one homeless person after another, and I see a great deal of suffering. Many homeless people report that they feel invisible. Since I don't want to shut down my heart, I carry an ample number of one-dollar bills in my wallet to give to certain homeless people as I walk by. I don't give to everyone, but to those I do, I offer kind wishes, and most of the time, they say, "God bless you."

The ER Doc

Medical burnout in the emergency room, especially for ER docs, is a well-known problem. The ER doc has enormous responsibilities to care for people in crisis, experiencing a lot of pain. This is especially true during worldwide pandemics. Many patients arrive past their point of recovery, even though an attempt to resuscitate is called for. These docs and nurses experience what is called "empathic distress." They feel the pain of their patients though the suffering takes a toll. Since compassion training is now known to make a positive difference and move people from empathy to compassion, many ER physicians and nurses are now practicing this kind of training.[85] Once established that compassion is a valuable part of medical practice, many healthcare professionals begin to enjoy both a more positive connection with their patients and greater resilience. Their compassion training breaks them out of their conditioned responses.

Breaking Our Conditioned Responses

A horse suddenly came galloping quickly down the road. It seemed as though the man had somewhere important to go. Another man standing alongside the road shouted, "Where are you going?" and the man on the horse replied, "I don't know! Ask the horse!"[86]

In this well-known Zen story, the horse represents our conditioned responses that our genetic makeup and our experiences have established. When our conditioned responses are having us respond to people or events in ways that aren't working for us, we need to pull the reins on our horse, get off, and take a deep breath. The doctors, who realized that their conditioned responses weren't working for them and were creating a painful experience, decided to make the changes in their lives through compassion training, were able to transform their work from being horrible into a positive situation.

During his life, the famous American author, Henry David Thoreau, a Transcendentalist, worried that he would find himself on his deathbed, only to realize that he had gone through life unconscious – and wasn't really living life. He was concerned that his old, conditioned responses would prevent him from being in the here and now and unable to experience reality. Every day he worked on staying awake and aware of his sensations and his feelings. In 1845, when he walked around Walden Pond, where he lived for two years, he wouldn't walk along the existing footpaths because he wanted to hear the leaves and the twigs making snapping sounds as he walked on them. He wanted the sounds to keep his attention in the present moment. He knew that it was the present moment where life, love and compassion can be experienced. The search for the means to overcome the ego-mind continued for ages. It's really the major challenge we all face all of the time.

Conclusion

By loving, you can then be love. The same is true for compassion. You can express compassion, and then you can be compassion. Compassion is a portal into our Higher Self, a doorway to our true nature, an opening into life. Through the compassion meditations, remember that any progress you are experiencing is a function of your stronger connections with your Higher Self. Once you are able to rest there, you naturally will become more compassionate. As a result, the people close to you will be lucky to have you in their lives because, when you become real, they will feel your compassion like they never did before.

Dr. Zach

Meditation:
And say to yourself silently:

- May I hold myself in compassion and understanding
- May my pain and sorrow be eased
- May my heart be at peace
- May I experience joy

And now say to yourself silently towards someone you care deeply about:

- May you be held in compassion and understanding
- May your pain and sorrow be eased
- May your heart be at peace
- May you experience joy.

10

Joy On Demand

Dr. Zach

The joy of Being, which is the only true happiness, can't come to you through any form, possession, achievement, person, or event – through anything that happens. That joy can't come to you – ever. It emanates from the formless dimension within you, from consciousness itself and thus is one with who you are.[87]

Eckhart Tolle, A New Earth

Tolle's "Being" is referring to our Higher Self. It's a shame that joy has been a rare occurrence. But when joy comes, it's glorious! Wouldn't it be great if we could create joy on demand in a gentle and loving way? Basically, almost any time? You might think this is impossible. My brother, who is quite spiritual, remarked about this possibility, "Good luck!" Let's learn some tools for bringing up joy on demand, however crazy that may sound.

This meditation series is about joy, inspired by Chade-Meng Tan's book *Joy on Demand*. Tan of Google fame.[88]

Even though Tan was so happy most of the time while he worked at Google, he actually lived a miserable life while growing up until he discovered meditation. Joy came to him through his practice and transformed him into a happy person. Inspired by his breakthrough book, it guided me to tailor this mindfulness series on joy.

Overview

Let's pause to review how far we have come before we look at what will follow. We have cultivated love through our loving-kindness meditation, peace of mind through breath awareness, and compassion through exercises on that theme. Now, we are covering joy. Chapter 11 will cover peace, and in Chapter 12, we will turn to wisdom. These qualities all build sublime and wonderful states, which will be nurturing throughout our journey. A good image to describe our journey is of an upward spiral, which is continuously climbing as we cultivate each quality of the Higher Self.

Joy From the Inside Out

As previously discussed, joy is one of the five key spiritual characteristics of the Higher Self. Joy is inherent to our innate state of being. How cool is that! So, like love and compassion (which are also characteristics of the Higher Self), joy emanates from inside of you when you are deeply present. In our meditation, we may experience abundance and generosity; or, in our most loving state, we may be open to the moment with all of its possibilities. In such expansive states, it's likely that we will feel joy spilling out toward others. Interestingly, joy is tied to our involvement with others through love and compassion. Joy is experienced when we feel connected to a greater whole, beyond ourselves. When we reach out to others in a compassionate way, we experience more of who we truly are. In turn, the other components of our Higher

Self come to fruition, like buds opening into blossoms consistent with Dr. Fredrickson's "broaden and build" theory.[89]

A Meditation to Generate Joy

In our mindfulness meditations, breathing exercises can lead into states of joy. Here is a meditation practice along these lines.

> **Meditation:**
> Take those three gentle breaths while breathing relaxation throughout your body. Now, wish someone you know to be happier. If you feel a little tingling in your body arising, that is joy, bring your full attention to that joy. Offer up your beautiful smile to keep the joy alive if you'd like to.

Joy: Our Natural State

Joy is the state that we experience when we open ourselves to the whole play of existence. Joy is a wonderful part of our Higher Self.

Remember that joy, like other natural states, isn't an emotion. The constant conditions of our Higher Self may be confused with emotions, which come and go in response to stimuli; however, our natural states are, in fact, ever present. We only periodically experience their presence because our fear-based ego-mind mainly dominates our awareness. It's only when an emotional moment overwhelms the ego-mind does an event momentarily crack open that veil that we get to experience our Higher Self. Unfortunately, the veil of fear quickly returns because our ego-mind demands to maintain full attention all of the time.

Our inner work brings our core states into awareness. They have mainly been kept in the dark for much of our lives. The neural pathway receivers associated with our Higher Self are forgotten and lie dormant. Like a plant that is kept in a closet for a long time, our Higher Self may seem to have wilted and dried up. Through meditation, we re-water the plant and revitalized the beneficial nerve pathways. Through the light of awareness, these qualities are replenished and energized. Then joy can become a normal part of our lives as we cultivate it by easing into joy.

Joy on demand is about tapping into the wellspring of joy that resides within us. This experience of joy is without sensual or ego stimulation. This is stimulus-free joy. Our meditation has three points of focus:

1) *Easing into Joy*: The first precondition for joy is a state of ease or peace; furthermore, you may become joyful that you are in a state of ease. Ease and joy reinforce each other. Peace also reinforces joy.

2) *Inclining towards Joy*: Here we notice and give our full attention to joy. We may do so during a calming breath or within everyday experiences. We become familiar with joy, as if joy were a close family

member, on whom we can count. The more the mind becomes familiar with joy, the more it perceives joy and inclines towards joy. In doing so, we effortlessly create the conditions conducive to joy. Similarly, we familiarize the mind with joy by welcoming, staying open, spending time, paying careful attention, and getting to know joy.

3) *Uplifting the Mind*: Here, we learn to uplift the mind by wholesome joy, especially joy arising from loving-kindness and compassion. The wholesomeness of such joy benefits our mental health as healthy food benefits our physical health. Such joy also leads the mind into a stable, collected state. The mind doesn't have to fight with contrary tendencies, like regret or envy. In turn, the sound, collected mind is conducive to wholesome joy. You can establish a virtuous cycle this way.

Good Vibrations

Ever since I have been practicing joy on-demand throughout my day, I have had trouble figuring out how to describe my feelings of gentle joy. Then all of sudden, a song by the Beach Boys, released in 1966, came to mind: "Good Vibrations." That was it. I was able to realize that my feelings of joy gently cause a vibration sensation in my body. Here are the lyrics.

Good Vibrations
by the Beach Boys

Embracing Your Higher Self

Verse 1
I love the colorful clothes she wears
And the way the sunlight plays upon
her hair
I hear the sound of a gentle word
On the wind that lifts her perfume
through the air

Chorus

I'm pickin' up good vibrations
She's giving me excitations
I'm pickin' up good vibrations
Good vibrations,
She's giving me excitations
Good, good, good, good vibrations

Close my eyes, she's somehow closer
now
Softly smile, I know she must be kind
When I look in her eyes
She goes with me to a blossom world

Ahh
Ah, my my, what elation
I don't know where but she sends me
there
Oh, my my, what a sensation
Oh, my my, what elation
Gotta keep those lovin' good vibrations
a-happenin' with her

Dr. Zach

Na na na na na, na na na

Hopefully, this song will get you to feel good vibrations if you are old enough to remember this sound. It was a giant hit. This is a spoiler alert, in the first meditation of the Joy on Demand series, I play a small clip from the song!

> **Meditation:**
> I invite you again to take three gentle deep breaths as you breathe relaxation throughout your body. Now, wish another person you know to be happier. If you feel a little tingling in your body arising, that is joy (good vibrations). Bring your full attention to that joy. Offer up your beautiful smile to keep the joy alive, if you'd like to. And now take three gentle deep breaths.

We are shaped by our thoughts; we become what we think. When the mind is pure, joy follows like a shadow that never leaves.

Buddha

We have our work cut out for us. However, joy is available to us at almost any time and can be just a few breaths away.

The more you incline your mind toward joy in real life, the more joyful and productive

*your meditations will tend to be. The more
you practice mindfulness, the more likely you
will be able to down-regulate habituation on
the strength of your mindfulness and enjoy
the pleasures of the day anew.*[90]

Chade-Meng Tan

Types of Joy

Let us clearly define joy and its related sources. There are a few types of joy. The first type relates to momentary emotions such as gladness. They occur when we discover something new or novel or make something new happen. These emotions come and go, as do all emotional responses. The second kind of joy is rapture, an elevation of our state of mind, sometimes referred to as "energetic joy." The third type, gentle joy, is a non-energetic joy, sometimes equated with happiness, bliss, or gentle well-being. It's the type of joy that leaves you contented. Rapture and gentle joy aren't true emotions, but they are drawn or sourced from the Higher Self. They present themselves whenever we access our Higher Self. When we are fully present and fully focused, we experience joy, especially when we attend to it. Through spiritual practice, we learn to awaken to our true nature.

An illustration of the first type of joy, a sort of gladness, happened one morning as I was sitting down with a wonderful plate of two eggs over easy, with avocado slices on top. Just as I was finishing my breakfast, I was overcome with a great sense of joy. This gladness caught me by surprise. Another type of joy, the non-energetic kind, arose as I put my full attention onto my feelings. I was present as I took a full deep breath. Then I breathed again, which brought relaxation to my whole body. Feeling compassionate, I wished my oldest daughter would be happier. This wish generated more joy, and the joy persisted. I put on a big smile, feeling it in the muscles around my eyes so that my joy would continue. Finally, as my attention faded, the joy faded as well. Thus, I experienced two types of joy within this single, joyous event at breakfast.

Joy Comes from Within:
An Illustration

Here is a well-known story about a man who was one night crawling around on his hands and knees to look for something underneath a lamppost. When his friends saw him, they asked him what he was looking for, and he told them that he had lost the key to his house. They all got down to help him look, without any success. Finally, one of them asked him where exactly he had lost the key, and he replied, "In the house." "Then why are you looking underneath the lamppost?"

The man replied, "Because there's more light here."

We are no different from this man. We are doing the same thing all of the time, always seeking fulfillment in sense pleasures, because we are being sold and then believing that having material things is where we will find happiness. But is it? We are learning that joy can be found from within and from just the simple wonders each day brings, at almost every moment, if we are only aware and attend to them.

Joy on Demand and the Happiness Set Point

Meditation is equivalent to mental calisthenics. The *Joy on Demand* meditations are like joy calisthenics. We can train ourselves to become joyful and move our happiness set point from a negative or neutral setting to a positive one. The happiness set point is our default setting for our sense of well-being. The default represents a fixed average level of happiness or unhappiness around which our day-to-day happiness varies. Our natural temperament is generally stable, while slowly moving moods and momentary changes are experienced as emotions and thoughts. This happiness set point is so powerful that people return to it after certain surprising and positive gains once the initial euphoria has died down, such as winning the lottery.

With regard to negative events, the set point is similarly reliable. People with serious spinal cord injuries return to their prior happiness set point after adjusting to the shock of their new and debilitating physical handicaps. The adjustment may take some months but eventually the initial set point returns.[91]

Dr. Zach

It's generally true that happiness set points establish a person's quality of life. The constancy is maintained because most people are constrained and imprisoned by their conditioned responses that don't change. They usually are influenced by childhood traumas and family patterns of behavior. However, we are experiencing and learning that meditation has the power to change those conditioned responses and thus change our happiness set points. Chade-Meng Tan offers living proof that meditation can cause a significant upgrade to one's happiness set point.

I experienced those benefits. I always thought I was a happy person until I started to meditate regularly. Based on my happiness set point, I realized that I was not as happy as I thought I was. There was a background mood of fear and self-doubt that permeated my consciousness and kept bringing me down. How was it that I was unaware? The basic moods, within which we live our lives, are like the water in which fish swim. Does a fish know it's swimming in water? Absolutely not, because water is all that it knows. The happiness set point indicates the quality of the water in which we swim. It's an integral part of who we think we are. It's part of our identity. Through meditation and self-awareness, I learned to recognize my happiness set point and to monitor it. My set point started moving in a more favorable direction, significantly, as I maintained a more positive state of being. Through my practice of this joy series of meditations, I shifted my set point to an even more favorable level.

The practice of inclining towards joy, which we discussed earlier, can be beneficial in creating new emotional habits. Ultimately, these habits can also affect our happiness set point. We notice the inclinations toward joy, and they increase when we give them our full attention. The following text is from Tan's book, *Joy on Demand*:

> *A beautiful description of our mental inclination is found in some ancient texts. Such inclinations are compared to mountain slopes. When the ground is sloped in a certain way, water flows effortlessly according to the direction of inclination. Similarly, when the mind is inclined in a certain way, thoughts and emotions happen effortlessly according to the nature of their inclination. If the mind is inclined toward joy, for example, then joyful thoughts and feelings tend to occur effortlessly. This simple but critically important insight leads to an equally important practical implication: the skillful way to train the mind isn't to exert forceful control over the mind itself, but rather to change its inclination so that thoughts and emotions occur effortlessly in the direction that one intends.*[92]

The inclination Tan is referring to is supported by a meditation practice. It can't be achieved through wrestling with your thoughts or trying hard to think the right thoughts. Thoughts just arise that you can't control. The change in your happiness set point will have a huge impact on the thoughts that do arise.

The happiness set point also involves our capacity to hold and transmute difficult experiences. This capacity will be the subject of our next series of meditations. As we learn to hold our struggles, and the struggles of others, within a place of joy and well-being, we develop a strong foundation for our happiness set point. This skill generally prevents us from falling into the depths of negativity, and if we find ourselves spiraling downwards, we can come back up more quickly.

Creating Our Reality

That we can be co-creators of our reality is hard to fathom. We so often blame outside factors for the quality of our lives: our parents, siblings, bosses, the times we live in, the government we are stuck with, and many other things. To blame is part of our conditioned response to our life situation. When we let our conditioned responses continue to rule our lives, we prevent ourselves from becoming free to make our own choices; we remain imprisoned and powerless. In such an unfree condition, we hardly feel like creators of our destiny; instead, it can seem that a straitjacket confines us. We are then ready to scream out in pain and frustration when things don't go our way.

Inclining Our Minds to Joy

It's hard to fathom that our Higher Self is joyful, and the joy stems from being alive and conscious. It then follows that virtually any event can generate joy. By becoming fully conscious of the possibilities within each moment, even in the most trying situations, we can become fully present by doing our breathing exercises, inclining our minds towards joy, and then letting our joyful selves be present. As a mountain slope guides a river effortlessly downstream, so joy may carry us toward better choices and, ultimately, to a more positive reality. This process provides an example of how we have the power to manage our reality. We learn how to be conscious of our freedom, make choices, and finally, do it. And we can, especially, incline toward joy right now.

Meditation:
I now invite you to take three gentle breaths as you breathe relaxation throughout your body. Now, wish someone you have some major issues with to be happy. If you feel a little tingling in your body arising, that is joy. Bring your full attention to that joy. Offer up your beautiful smile to keep the joy alive, if you'd like to.

Joy and Suffering

We turn now to the second part of our Joy on Demand meditation series. Here we deal with some seemingly contradictory factors. We will discover that joy isn't simply a fleeting mood of gladness, jubilation, or euphoria. It can be a force for healing and well-being in helping people in pain and suffering, whether their afflictions be temporary or chronic and intense.

It can be nice to feel great and to say, "I feel great!" but a deep sense of joy runs deeper. Joy lifts you and others when you are feeling down and out. In the joy meditations, the meditator is asked to be attentive to joyful and uplifting forces, even while experiencing the pain of someone close. It's relevant to experience joy during emotional pain and allow that joy to surface whenever and wherever it likes. Additionally, we cultivate the willingness to experience the emotional pain of others. This ability is a key tool for helping make use of joy to temper and heal that pain.

Underlying war is peace, underlying hatred is love, underlying coldness is compassion, and underlying deep suffering is joy. Our Higher Self can embrace these contrary attributes. Joy isn't a fleeting experience of exhilaration but instead a key and vibrant component of our true nature as well as another portal to our Higher Self. This joy is ready to emerge when we are suffering so that we can heal.

Joy to Alleviate Grief

Over a recent conversation with a friend, I explained that "joy on demand" can involve holding grief within a state of joy. My friend looked at me as if I had two heads. In our core nature, I explained, we are joyful beings. And even when we are in a state of grief, our inner joy is never extinguished. Joy can be curative when we are grieving. We will soon dive more deeply into this dynamic. The Dalai Lama tells this story of a certain Tibetan monk, who had spent more than eighteen years in a Chinese prison labor camp.

> *This monk told me that on a few occasions he really faced some danger. So, I asked him, "What danger? What kind of danger?" thinking he would tell me of Chinese torture and prison. He replied, "Many times I was in danger of losing my compassion for the Chinese."*[93]

Just as this monk made use of his innate compassion to overcome his tendency to hate his jailors and to deal with his pain, so we can make use of our innate joy to alleviate our grieving, no matter how intense our grief may be. We may draw upon our inner joy to help us to heal.

The Stories We Tell Ourselves

The stories we tell ourselves shape the way we live our lives. If this is true, we would surely tell ourselves a better story if we had the choice. Do we have the power to choose a better life storyline? Of course, the answer is yes! The first step in doing so is to become aware of our conditioned existence. Through our joy exercises, we then create joy where it hadn't previously existed within our consciousness. We unlock the joy part of ourselves through self-compassion. Our newly found ability to make choices provides a wonderful way, step by step, to create a more joyful existence. We then make use of these tools via guided meditations to become authors of a renewed reality.

Joy: The Treasure Within

Tolle tells the following story:[94]

A beggar had been sitting by the side of a road for over thirty years. One day a stranger walked by. "Spare some change?" mumbled the beggar, mechanically holding out his old baseball cap.

"I have nothing to give you," said the stranger. Then he asked: "What's that you are sitting on?"

"Nothing," replied the beggar. "Just an old box. I have been sitting on it for as long as I can remember."

"Ever looked inside?" asked the stranger.

"No," said the beggar. "What's the point? There's nothing in there."

"Have a look inside," insisted the stranger.

The beggar managed to pry open the lid. With astonishment, disbelief and elation, he saw that the box was filled with gold.

This parable describes the dilemma and struggles we find ourselves in at every moment. The box of gold represents our Higher Self which is available to us anytime. But unfortunately, our beggar mentality is driven by our faulty ego-mind's sense of self and keeps us from doing our inner work. The ego-mind keeps us searching for physical gifts with the illusory claim that we will become happy by satisfying our earthly needs. Remember the ego-mind doesn't want us to look inside ourselves because it will be found out! So, when it starts to squawk and complain about doing inner work, just ignore it.

Acres of Diamonds

Another fascinating story demonstrates how the most significant treasure exists right inside us and how we continually believe that our search for happiness is somewhere out there, outside of ourselves in physical objects. Over a century ago, Russell Conwell became famous for his traveling lecture, entitled *Acres of Diamonds*.[95] He gave this talk over 6,000 times, making him one of the most original and well-known motivational speakers.

There was once a wealthy man named Ali Hafed who lived not far from the River Indus in Iraq. He was contented because he was wealthy, and wealthy because he was contented. One day, a priest visited Ali Hafed and told him all about diamonds. And how much they were worth. He went to his bed that night a poor man. He had not lost anything, but he was poor because he was discontented, and discontented because he feared he was poor. Ali Hafed sold his farm, left his family, and traveled to Palestine and then to Europe, searching for diamonds. He didn't find them. His health and his wealth failed him. Dejected, he cast himself into the sea.

One day, the man who had purchased Ali Hafed's farm found a curious sparkling stone in a stream that cut through his land. It was a diamond. Digging produced more diamonds - acres of diamonds, in fact. This, according to the parable, was the discovery of the famed diamonds of Golconda. By the end of the 19th century, the Golconda market was the primary source of the finest and largest diamonds in the world.

In *Acres of Diamonds*, Ali Hafed was a relatively wealthy person. But he began to feel poor hearing how wealthy he could become owning a diamond mine, His failure to find additional riches drove him to suicide. Abundance is a mindset without envy or craving. He was unable to find the gold coins in the box he was sitting on all day long. He also failed to discover the joy his life could offer him if he only looked inside.

The Kitchen Faucet

I experienced my craving more recently when I installed a new kitchen faucet. At first, I took great pride and enjoyment in how it looked. It was sleek and modern, and it could shoot out a strong spray. Then, one day I was visiting a friend, and when I went into his kitchen to wash some fruit, I noticed that his faucet began spraying as soon as it turned on. Mine at home required me first to lift the handle and then press a button under its neck to turn on the spray. All of a sudden, I wasn't experiencing joy in my new faucet. It seemed inferior like it wasn't as good as my friend's. The faucet still looked modern and gave me a strong spray, and I had installed it myself! All the other conditions were the same. But now the joy was gone. A new factor had entered in: a craving for more, combined with a mindset of comparison and competition.

Research shows that we are hardwired to notice negatives in this way once our expectations are aroused to make comparisons with something better.[96]

Yet, luckily, we have spiritual tools to counteract this unfortunate response. So, I set out to rewire my brain through a combination of breathing, gratitude exercises and connecting with my awareness of joy. Every time I used my faucet, I would breathe in a sense of gratitude towards my new faucet, breathe out my negative feelings, and feel the sense of joy. It worked! I'm now back to fully enjoying my new faucet again.

> **Meditation:**
> I now invite you to take three gentle deep breaths while breathing relaxation throughout your body. Think of one thing you are grateful for and breathe into that thought. Now feel if you have any feeling of a good vibration emerging. You can now relax.

The faucet story is an example of the power of our spiritual techniques. Using the breath, gratitude, and joy on demand, we can rewire our brains in everyday life; we are like brain electrical engineers. We can use these tools to liberate ourselves from our natural hardwiring and negative conditioned responses.

Conclusion

Joy and suffering go well together in a totally unsuspecting way. Joy is like the last thing you would think would be linked to hardship. When I was working on helping to create peace in the Middle East and was working with the Israelis and Palestinians conducting bridge-building and peacemaking workshops, I was struck by how often the Palestinians would laugh. I would eventually interpret this behavior as a way for them to deal with their suffering.

Embracing Your Higher Self

When the body is injured and starts to bleed, amazing things happen as the body stops the blood loss and heals itself. The same thing happens with our consciousness when we experience emotional pain, and our inner joy emerges to heal us.

It's good to remember that joy at times can be loud and boisterous, but mostly it emerges as a good vibration that needs great sensitivity and heightened self-awareness to sense it.

We have reached another significant milestone. We have experienced and practiced joy and the ability to create it and make it part of our lives. Our next topics will be inner peace and then wisdom. The path you are on provides you with the essential abilities to activate the components of your Higher Self at will. Over time, you will begin to combine these elements into a fully integrated, holistic experience of your Higher Self. Most significantly, you will be fully present and sustain that presence. You will learn to operate from the space of your Higher Self, for a significant portion of your life. That is our key objective. That is what enlightenment is all about.

11

Peace Now

Embracing Your Higher Self

Imagine all the people living life in peace. You may say I'm a dreamer, but I'm not the only one. I hope someday you'll join us, and the world will live as one.

John Lennon, Imagine

All we are saying is give peace a chance.

John Lennon, Give Peace a Chance

This series is dear to my heart because I focused on creating peace in the world for most of my life. My experiments in peacemaking took many forms. There were marches, celebrations, conferences, demonstrations, retreats, and some meditation – but not enough meditation. It was years later that I realized inner peace mainly derives from meditation. Meditation is the wellspring for peace and peacemaking in the world.

Meditation is essential in the peacemaking process because peace comes from our Higher Self. When we experience this part of our Higher Self, we can project it out into our world, and peaceful things begin to happen all around us.

> **Meditation:**
> Sense your body right now. Now take three gentle breaths. Do you feel a bit more relaxed and peaceful? If so, you are tapping into the peace within you. Take three more deep gentle breaths and feel that peace.

Defining Peace

Peace on earth, goodwill to humanity. The ever-sought-after world peace, the dream of people everywhere. So, what is peace really? And from where does it come? Webster's dictionary (updated 2020) states: *it's a time of no war, a period of tranquility or quiet, a state of security within a community provided by law or custom and for the individual, harmony in personal relations, freedom from the disquieting or oppressive thoughts or emotions, at peace, in a state of tranquility.* The dictionary gives us a nice, holistic view of peace and nonviolence and inner quiet: globally, within each nation, in our communities, families, close personal relationships, and inside ourselves.

In Jack Kornfield's *The Wise Heart*, he describes practices for developing pure consciousness. These can provide a foundation for meditations geared toward peace.[97]

Develop a mind that is vast like space,
where experiences both pleasant and
unpleasant can appear and disappear without

conflict, struggle, or harm. In college, I tried a little meditation on my. But I was unsuccessful because I didn't know what I was doing. It wasn't that I was afraid of silence or of some terrible darkness that I would find inside, though these are common misunderstandings of meditation. It was that my body would get uncomfortable and my mind would spin out in a million directions.

When a respected meditation teacher helped me figure things out, the practice became gradually clearer. He taught me to relax and feel my breath carefully, which helped focus and quiet my mind. Then he taught me just to mindfully notice the stream of thoughts and sensations without reacting to them as a problem. This took some practice. Finally, he taught the most important lesson, to rest in consciousness itself.

He said, "We can notice the distinction between consciousness and all the transient states and experiences that arise and pass away within it. When we don't understand this point, we take each of the passing states to be real. But when changing conditions such as happiness and unhappiness are seen for what they are, we find the way to peace. If you can rest in the knowing, the pure consciousness, you have accomplished a lot."

Peace: Quieting the Ego-Mind

Struggling to write this section, I looked over different books while scanning the web. I made false starts at writing, only to stop short. I just couldn't find my rhythm. I was frustrated. Appropriately, I decided to meditate. I quieted my cognitive mind to let my Higher Self and inner wisdom take over. Instantly, an insight came to me on how best to proceed with this section. Presence is the only way to experience life. My frustration arose when I tried to let my ego-mind figure something out that required my Higher Self. The ego-mind knows nothing about the Higher Self as its source of wisdom. Once I became fully present, the answer came right to me and put a smile on my face. I received proof illustrating the anecdote about the beggar (presented in Chapter 10). I became that beggar sitting on that wooden box, filled with gold coins. I was holding out a cup, asking people for some change, while a treasure chest of insights was already available to me; this is true for you, too.

We can easily tie ourselves into knots and feel like we are incapable of breaking free. Our ego-mind often tries to lock us up within its limited perspective of reality. On so many levels, this perspective is flawed. The daily habit of doing our inner work is essential for wresting ourselves free from its grip. Willpower is unreliable, for the ego-mind will undercut it. A consistent meditation habit will reign supreme by helping us keep our ability to embrace our Higher Self consistent.

The following story illustrates how the mind can become peaceful.[98]

> *Once Buddha was walking from one town to another with a few of his followers. This was in the initial days. While they were traveling, they happened to pass a lake. They stopped there and Buddha told one of his disciples, "I'm thirsty. Do get me some water from that lake there."*

> *The disciple walked up to the lake. When he reached it, he noticed that some people were washing clothes in the water and, right at that moment, a bullock cart started crossing through the lake. As a result, the water became very muddy, very turbid. The disciple thought, "How can I give this muddy water to Buddha to drink!" He came back and told Buddha, "The water in there is very muddy. I don't think it's fit to drink."*

> *After about half an hour, again Buddha asked the same disciple to go back to the lake and get him some water to drink. The disciple obediently went back to the lake. This time he found that the lake had absolutely clear water in it. The mud had settled down, and the water above it looked fit to be had. So, he collected some water in a pot and brought it to Buddha. Buddha looked at the water, and then he looked up at the disciple and said,*

Dr. Zach

*"See what you did to make the water clean.
You let it be ... and the mud settled down on
its own – and you got clear water... Your
mind is also like that. When it's disturbed,
just let it be. Give it a little time. It will settle
down on its own. You don't have to put in any
effort to create peace of mind because that
peace is inside of you. It will happen. It's
effortless."*

Meditation:
Let's do a nice breath awareness exercise to become
more peaceful. I invite you to count to ten with
counting the first inhalation as #1 and the following
exhalation as #2 and so on until you get to #10. If you
get lost in thought just pick up with the last number
you can remember and continue to count to #10.

Breath Awareness: Quieting the Ego-mind, Creating Peace of Mind

The beauty of our meditation is that it allows us
to center ourselves within the reality of the present
moment. Unfortunately, our ego-minds keep pulling us
out of being fully present. It tries hard to keep our
attention by continuously focusing our awareness
towards the past (by regretting or ruminating) or
towards the future (by fearing, planning, or
daydreaming). The ego-mind takes on an imaginary
sense of self and operates in a make-believe world

trapping us into the past and future. Since the present moment is the only true reality, and the ego-mind can't function in reality, it needs to steer us away from it. Hence, the ego-mind is draining and creates a life of struggle, mainly creating a tug-of-war between our illusory-based ego-mind and our Higher Self in trying to dominate our consciousness. Peace of mind occurs when we can establish order within our two minds; that will happen when we develop the ability to have our Higher Self become the master of our consciousness, and the ego-mind becomes its servant.

The ego-mind plays a valuable and positive role when it isn't trying to make us believe it's our Higher Self. The ego-mind has executive functions described by Maslow's hierarchy of needs: physiological needs (food, water, warmth, rest, and shelter); safety needs (security and protection); belonging needs; and satisfying our need for esteem. But we now know the ego-mind does many things that interfere with our desire for enlightenment because it's a false sense of self. It's clearly out of bounds and harmful playing this role.

However, the ego (as opposed to the ego-mind) does have a positive role to play, using its executive functions to set down guidelines for what is appropriate and what isn't because our Higher Self tends to give everything away. The Higher Self has great power to connect with everyone from a love perspective, and the ego will help modulate the Higher Self's overreaching tendencies. Even though the ego has certain essential parts to play in helping us stay alive and well, it doesn't help us reach out to others from the heart nor connecting with spiritual reality on any level.

When the ego-mind dominates our consciousness, there no inner peace nor resulting peacemaking because the emotion underlying the ego-mind is fear, not love.

Again, the essential method to transition from the ego-mind to the Higher Self is to use our trusty tool – breath awareness. It grounds us in the present moment. We can then draw upon the power of our inner peace, another characteristic of our Higher Self. From there, we can experience peace and start projecting it out to others. Through the power of resonance, this inner peace vibrates peace all around us, on all levels and without limit.

Model for an Enlightened Peaceful Life: The River

In the Peace Now series, I introduce a guided visualization of living life on a river that helps the meditator experience peace while dealing with life's struggles. This experiential visual model utilizes the dynamics of three components: the ego-mind, the Higher Self, and life itself. To begin, let's imagine a river that emerges from a spring, way up in the mountains. The spring comes from purified well water, deep in the bowels of mother earth. The river starts with a robust flow of clean mountain water and then moves down toward the sea, through canyons and valleys, until it finally empties into a large bay. The river loses some of its physical form as it merges into the larger body of water.

The river symbolizes the course of our life. The water emanating from the mountain spring represents our birth. Initially, we float down the river in a small canoe. As the river becomes wider and we grow into adulthood, we start traveling down the river on two totally different larger vessels: a houseboat and a life raft. The riding along on the houseboat symbolizes the time in our life when we are being consumed by our ego-mind. When traveling on the life raft, this represents experiencing life through our Higher Self.

The river, houseboat, and life raft represent our physical and spiritual life. We are constantly flowing down the river until we end up in the sea, representing the death of our body but not our Higher Self or soul.

The image of a "life raft" (our Higher Self) was chosen to suggest that, to experience life to the fullest, you need a rescue vehicle (the life raft) to get out of the houseboat (our ego-mind). With our life raft, we can periodically escape the houseboat, which has, up to this point, helped us through life. But, from here on out, we want to move on locked up in a troubling state and find peace by learning to ride down the river of life primarily in our life raft.

When we are in our ego-mind, we are on the houseboat, which isn't pleasant. Do you remember the line "a house isn't a home?" A house only becomes a home when there is love in it. Since the ego-mind is devoid of love, the houseboat remains a house, not a home. First off, this houseboat is a bit unusual because it has a high fence all around the outside edge of the boat. It's so high that the captain, who is you, can't see the river over the fence, nor how it flows nor its direction. When we are in our ego-mind, we disconnect from the flow of our lives and constantly think about things in the past or the future. Our inability to be present is represented by our inability to see the river above the high fence. When we don't see the river, we are unaware of where we are going or how to steer our boat. We are in a fog. Thankfully, there is always a direction to our lives that continues independently, regardless of how we try to steer our houseboat consciously. This is represented by the power and flow of the river. There is a wisdom that exists in the flow of the river and affects our lives, even if we can't directly access it or see it from the perspective of our ego-mind.

We become peaceful when we steer right into the flow or direction of the river. That is when we are in the "flow." When we steer with the river's "current," we are fully present, in the here and now, and that is the key to experiencing peace. Unfortunately, when we are on the houseboat, it's almost impossible to be in the flow because we cannot see the ever-changing direction of the currents.

There are times, while in our ego-mind, we try to accept certain events and ride with them, but fear takes us over, and we withdraw from the "current" moment and lose the ability to be fully present. That is what happens on the houseboat; we are disconnected from reality and can't see the currents in the river to steer into the flow because the high fence of fear and lack of presence prevents us from doing so. We end up steering blind.

Luckily, our houseboat attaches to our life raft by a rope. And whenever we start meditating, we magically are lifted off the houseboat then gently settle into our warm, soft, love-filled, transparent inflatable life raft. Being so pliable, we sink into the life raft as it form-fits around our legs, hips, and lower back, allowing us to sit comfortably upright. From here, we can experience our inner peace and the flow of life as it carries us along. In our life raft, we experience life to its fullest. Or, as Lao Tzu referred to it, *The Way of Life*.[99]

Sitting in our life raft, without a fence around us, we can observe the river, the flow of life, experiencing the spiritual realm, and feeling peace being at one with the river. Since the life raft is transparent, we can look down and through the life raft into the river's depths and experience the essence of life itself. The life raft is light and flexible, it just effortlessly finds the currents and moves with them as they change direction or speed up, moment by moment.

> **Meditation:**
> Take your nice three gentle breaths. Now, imagine you are on your warm, light, pliable life raft as you gently flow down the river with the sun shining, and you lean back, feeling very peaceful. Now take three more gentle deep breaths while you do so.

In great contrast, when we are back on the houseboat, it generates turbulence as it spins around as we try to navigate along the river without really seeing our way along. Unable to sense the currents, we bump up against one current after another, going this way and that. Similarly, in real life, our ego-minds keep avoiding the present moment by generating a storm of thoughts, emotions, moods, and physical sensations, disconnecting us from reality. Unfortunately, we are unable to feel them because we aren't in the present moment.

To clarify, the high fence around the houseboat allows us to recognize physical but not spiritual things. The only physical things we see are the banks of the river but not the river itself. By "spiritual," I mean the life energies or life forces that make up who we are as well as the life energies of other people and the world around us. When we are in our ego-minds and on the houseboat, we are unaware of our lives' spiritual aspects, resulting in feeling disconnected, separate from others, and even from ourselves.

Our Objective

As we have seen, the river model is a good practical way to understand the dynamics we experience when we make transitions from our ego-mind to our Higher Self and back again. The objective is to reside most of our day within our Higher Self and use our ego-mind when it's appropriate. In the river analogy, we can then let the houseboat trail behind us as we lead the way down the river in our life raft when the houseboat isn't needed. When you master this, you will achieve peace of mind.

You may have realized by now, it's a wonderful experience being in the Higher Self. It's the place where we would rather be most of the time. It's our destiny to become grounded in the Higher Self. Then when we need executive functions, we can shift back into the ego-mind. Once done with the ego-mind, we can go right back to the Higher Self. The objective of our journey is to be able to make those shifts deftly. Part of this process is making friends with the ego-mind.

Meditation and World Peace

The day the power of love overrules the love of power, the world will know peace.

Mahatma Gandhi

This quote by Gandhi ties in with Chade-Meng Tan in his first book, *Search Inside Yourself.*[100] Besides being one of Google's earliest programmers, he also had a job as the company's Jolly Good Fellow, who would welcome VIP guests when they visited the Google headquarters. Tan also organized the Google mindfulness program, the most popular of Google's extracurricular classes. Meng's life goal is to bring about world peace by spreading inner peace and compassion through meditation, which he feels is the major component in facilitating that transition. It's my belief and goal in life to spread meditation to as many people as I can. We have come to the same conclusion.

The following describes a eureka moment Tan had while he was still at Google:

Everybody already has a rough idea of what emotional intelligence is. More importantly, everybody knows that emotional intelligence is a beneficial skill. Even without fully understanding EQ, many people know or suspect that EQ will help them fulfill their worldly goals in life. Such as becoming more effective at work, getting promotions, earning more money, working more effectively with other people, being admired and having fulfilling relationships. In other words, EQ aligns perfectly with the needs and desires of modern life. It has two more important features. First, beyond helping us succeed, EQ can increase our inner happiness, empathy, and compassion for people, precisely what we need for world peace. Second, a very good way (and I suspect the only way) to truly develop EQ is with contemplative practices, starting with meditation.

Eureka! I found it! The way to create the conditions for world peace is to create a mindfulness-based emotional intelligence curriculum, perfect it within Google, and then give it away as one of Google's gifts to the world. The alignment is perfect. Everybody already wants EQ, businesses already want EQ, and we can help them achieve it. They can then become more effective at achieving their own goals and at the same time create the foundations for world peace.[101]

When I read this section in Tan's book, I couldn't believe it. It was exactly my thought. I feel that potentially the most powerful force for positive change in the world is combining the profit-making machinery (corporations) with the power of meditation and how it can create enlightened workforces. When the business community realizes that a meditating company can help it become more profitable, more and more companies will integrate meditation into the work experience. This corporate wave of positive change can go a long way in transforming the world. After I finish this book, I promise you I will reach out to Tan and discuss how we can work together.

Dr. Zach

Why We Thirst for Peace in our Lives

Many people say to themselves when they are feeling extreme stress, "Please give me a break from this unsettling experience of living." When we live our lives stuck in the ego-mind, so much of it's all about analyzing, comparing, fearing, regretting, and worrying. Plus, we find ourselves in this unpleasant bouncing back and forth between the past and the future.

Psychologically, we also tend to beat up on ourselves for not being good enough by playing back the scolding voices of our parents. Not to mention indulging our mind storms when we bombard ourselves with thousands of criticizing thoughts per day. Most of them are thoughts that keep repeating themselves. We become so exhausted we tend towards depression, just trying to deal with this constant bombardment. Therefore, it's vital to do an inner practice daily to give oneself a break from this cacophony. We all need more peace – peace of mind.

Even though we read how great life can be when you experience life from within the Higher Self, the ego-mind does a great job of convincing us that our "sense of separation from others" is our true nature. This false claim underpins the ego-mind. It keeps claiming to be our true and only self. This is the major illusion with which we are struggling. If the ego-mind were the Higher Self, then why would the ego-mind keep veering us away from being present? There is something seriously wrong with this picture. By contrast, our Higher Self can only function appropriately in the here and now, where everything really takes place. If you were a betting person, where would you put your money as to which is the real self? We need to send up the white flag and surrender so that we can have peace of mind. Surrender to this reality and accept that this is no way to live and make a firm commitment to start creating peace in your life, which is right here, waiting to happen.

Altered Trait

A critical objective for our practice is to achieve what is called an "altered trait," as opposed to an "altered state." An altered state, attained during meditation, lasts only a little while afterward. An altered trait, by contrast, is more lasting and rewires the brain. Thus, research about the "altered trait" is a good measure of the results of meditation in producing a centered state of being.[102]

One of the key altered traits generated through meditation is the increased resilience to stress shown to last for at least three months following a four-day meditation retreat.[103] When we activate our Higher Self, one of the principle spiritual characteristics, inner peace, is experienced. One of the special capabilities of inner peace is an increased resilience to stress. If you increase your ability to focus, concentrate and increase your resilience to stress, you will have two defenses to keep you on track to accomplish your goals in life and live a life in peace.

Conclusion: Peace

Peace is an essential part of who we are. The best way to experience peace is to rest in our awareness. We can find that place in our consciousness, where we are fully present to observe our thoughts, feelings, emotions, sensations, and moods from a place where there is peace. That place is when we are fully present in our Higher Self.

At our core, we are simply consciousness or awareness. In experiencing this, we can fully feel our inner peace. We can get there by using the power of our breath. When we are stressed, we tend to take shallow breaths. You may be stressed when you find yourself late to work; you immediately go into a state of fear, and unconsciously start taking shallow breaths and even sometimes holding your breath. These disruptions in breathing further increase your stress because you are choking yourself unconsciously. And that isn't pleasant. So, when you become aware that this is happening and take those delicious three deep breaths, you stimulate your vagal nerve (part of your parasympathetic nervous system). This mechanism tells your body that everything is okay; you can begin to relax and return to your natural breathing. Then you can experience some of that inner peace you have been connecting with during your practice. When you resonate with your inner peace, you can share this peace with others.

While resting in awareness, you can watch your emotions and thoughts come and go from a place of peace and centeredness. The key is to realize that you are the awareness itself rather than the passing emotions and thoughts. Your inner awareness is a constant. The primary tool to access your awareness is your breath, while your emotions and thoughts move on and new ones emerge. In this manner, you stay in a peaceful state. Peace is experienced more and more in your practice and your daily life. We will return to the topic of peace later on in our journey.

Meditation:
Sense your body right now. Take three gentle breaths while thinking about someone you care a lot about. Then say silently to this person after me:

I offer you peace.
I offer you love
I offer you friendship
I see your beauty
I hear your needs
I feel your feelings
My wisdom flows from the highest source
I salute that source in you
Let us work together… for unity and peace.

12

Wisdom On Demand

> *To experience more synchronicity and "coincidences" we need to listen and be aware of the world around us and also our intuition. That's how the universe speaks to itself; it's an ongoing flow of information that comes from both the outside and from within. Pay attention to how the universe speaks to you today and participate in the flow by being attentive and by listening to your inner voice.*[104]
>
> *Maria Erving,*
> *personal development coach*

What if I told you that wisdom isn't just about having learned from meaningful lifelong experiences? What if wisdom is understanding the ability to tap into the infinite wisdom available to all of us. Now that would be a twist!

There is no chance that I would have created this meditation journey if I weren't continually drawing upon our collective inner wisdom. The HMJ weaves many strands of knowledge and experiences into a vivid fabric, alive and vibrant. It draws upon intuitions, *aha* moments, and holistic insights. It's these diverse sources that make wisdom possible.

Wisdom Comes from Within: Gandhi

There is a famous story about Mahatma Gandhi and the salt tax. Gandhi used his inner wisdom and the power of meditation many times when he was leading the struggle for Indian independence from British rule. For almost 200 years, the British had instituted a salt tax on every Indian. The tax was so high that for many Indian citizens, it represented 15% of their annual income. The unfair tax required each person to buy all of their salt from a British company at an exorbitant price. The leaders of the Indian National Party came to visit Gandhi to ask him for a strategy on how to fight this ridiculous tax finally. Gandhi told them, "Let me meditate on this." He meditated for seven whole weeks before coming up with the strategy of a nonviolent march to the sea to harvest salt from the beaches in defiance of British law. Gandhi started with only a dozen followers. After marching 270 miles, he had attracted tens of thousands of followers when arriving at the sea. The 60-year-old Mahatma (meaning "the great soul," the honorific given to him by his followers), with the help of this demonstration, shook the foundations of British rule, which eventually led to India's independence.

Gandhi used the power of meditation to make a revolutionary political decision that changed the course of history. However, using meditation to help solve problems is nothing new. A lot of us say before answering a difficult question, "Let me meditate on that before I answer your question."

In ancient Greece, wisdom and insight were held in such high regard and occurred with such rarity people believed muses or Greek demi-gods had all the great ideas. As it was told, the muses, who lived on Mt. Olympus, would reach into their little vats and take out an idea and throw it down to the people. If you were a lucky target, they would hit you on the head with a great idea. Luckily, instead of going all the way up to Mt. Olympus for support, we can just go inside ourselves.

Accessing and Recording the Wisdom from the Higher Self

Previously in our meditations, we have been learning to distance ourselves from our thoughts. We imagine that they are just clouds floating by in a blue sky. We learn to let them float by without getting caught up in them. Our goal is to quiet the ego-mind, connect with the Higher Self, rest in awareness, and observe our thoughts rather than being caught up in our thoughts. In our wisdom meditations, we are going to do the complete opposite. We will interrupt our meditation to notice our ideas or thoughts immediately. The thoughts we find meaningful will be written down or recorded right away. These ideas may take different forms: they can be insights, thoughts, images, or hunches. The Higher Self sends us insights since it's always working behind the scenes on solving problems and providing valuable guidance. It's helpful to note if you don't record the guidance right away, you will forget it – similar to dreams, which you must record immediately upon awakening to remember them.

It's reasonable to ask, "So, why didn't we take notice of our thoughts in our past meditations?" It's because the key tool for accessing the Higher Self is to quiet the ego-mind first. In meditation, we don't want to allow the ego-mind to be active because, once the ego-mind starts revving up, we find ourselves no longer in a meditation state. So, exclusively, in this inner wisdom series, you will be noticing thoughts you believe are insights, recording them, and then going right back to your meditation. You won't reflect upon or explore the insights – just record them. After you finish your meditations, you can read over the wisdom and guidance you have received and decide what you want to do with them. To sort this out isn't an easy process, but you will get better at it as time goes on.

Here are some steps for recording your insights:

1. Keep a notepad right beside you to write down your insights.
2. Keep a notepad app open on your phone to record them.
3. I find the easiest thing to do is make a new note on your note app and use the voice recording feature to transcribe right into your note. The value of the voice memo technique is that you can minimize the disruption to your meditation to return right back to your meditation state. However, learning styles do vary. Some will prefer taking written notes; others will record memos.

Intuition

The ability to access the infinite wisdom within you is about developing skills for deepening your meditation and being present when an insight arises. With practice, these skills and benefits will all come together soon enough. There will be times when the meditations generate many insights and other times nothing. The intuitive mind doesn't work like the ego-mind.

We use the act of asking for answers in our practice to help the process. This is like prayer; some say it is prayer. However, if you sit there and push, push, push for answers, your effort will be unproductive. We are going deep into ourselves to experience who we are in our essence and feel out our Higher Self's differing characteristics. The Higher Self responds when you are fully present, and you will gain a sense of your inner wisdom through these meditations; you will be experiencing longer stretches of quiet, and those resources will open up to you.

Now, let me again be clear, just because you receive a thought, message, or image during a state of meditation, this doesn't mean its wisdom. It's just that wisdom thoughts best come to you when you are in a meditation state. After receiving these thoughts, it's your job to determine if they are meaningful, regardless of their origin. There are times when your state of meditation is interrupted, and your ego-mind starts operating, and the thoughts that emerge are from your ego-mind and not from your Higher Self. The thoughts from your Higher Self will come to you when you are in a consistent state of meditation.

Wisdom and Creativity

Many studies have shown that stress reduces creativity.[105] As you might have guessed, meditation is one of the best methods to increase resilience to stress. When you develop resilience, you can stay more relaxed so your creativity, which comes from your intuitive wisdom, can become more accessible. Einstein would pick up his violin to play Mozart when he faced a vexing problem; he couldn't solve the problem using his cognitive mind alone. Playing music was Einstein's form of meditation and his stress reduction technique. Our series, Wisdom on Demand, maximizes our ability to focus our attention to tap into our wisdom, which is the source of our creativity.

The Ego-mind: The False Self and Our Struggles

Our brain is a fantastic tool that resonates with the Higher Self and allows us to function on this physical plane. Scientists believe that our brains are the most unusual physical form in the universe.[106] However, our brains have given us a confusing scenario to deal with because we have a false sense of self (the ego-mind). Our Higher Self "waits" for the receiver in our brains and hearts to be brought to life. During that transition, we experience struggles and pain.

Where Does Our Wisdom Come From?

Today, many top scientists admit that they don't know where our sense of self or the center of awareness is located. One of the most famous neurosurgeons ever, Dr. Wilford Penfield, was a dualist. That means he believed the mind itself was separate from the physical brain. Actually, many neurosurgeons are dualists. Dr. Penfield's opinion is highly regarded because he was an expert in epilepsy, treating over 1,000 epileptic patients tortured by periodic seizures. He conducted surgery on epileptics to eliminate their seizures. Dr. Penfield performed the surgery under local anesthesia. He would cut open the roof of the skull so the top of the brain would be exposed while the patients were fully conscious throughout the procedure. The patients needed to be awake to help the surgeon map out different parts of the brain to determine exactly which specific locations in the brain incisions needed to be made. As a footnote, the brain doesn't experience pain.

Dr. Penfield would take electrodes and poke into different sites in the exposed brain while the patient would respond, indicating what they were experiencing from each individual poke. Dr. Penfield would make about two hundred pokes per procedure, meaning that he made over 200,000 pokes over his surgical career to evoke patients' responses. After this incredible amount of patient feedback and data, Dr. Penfield felt that the mind isn't solely in the brain but located outside of the brain. He concluded that certain powers, particularly the intellect and will, aren't generated by brain matter but from sources that aren't material. He believed the mind wasn't in the brain because after all of his poking around, he could never elicit from any of the patients a response related to intellectual functioning or will. He believed that the physical brain only generates physical perception, movement, and memory.[107]

There are two additional researchers who have built strong cases in support of the dualists position. Roger W. Sperry was a professor of psychobiology at the California Institute of Technology. Sperry won a Nobel Prize in physiology studying patients who had their two hemispheres surgically separated by severing the corpus callosum, the broad band of nerve fibers that connect the two hemispheres.[108] This was a radical surgical approach to treat people with epilepsy who were experiencing life-threatening seizures. Now, imagine this: the surgeon goes into your skull and separates the two hemispheres of your brain and your intellect and will, or soul or as we refer to as the Higher Self, is undivided! Sperry won his Nobel Prize studying these patients and found that there were few differences in patient performance before the brain was cut in half and afterward. In ordinary life, there was little difference. Sperry had to do meticulous studies to notice a difference before and after the surgery. The most remarkable result of Sperry's Nobel Prize-winning work was that the person's intellect and will – what we might call the soul – remained undivided. The brain can be cut in half, but the intellect and will can't.

Benjamin Libet, a researcher in physiology at the University of California, San Francisco, conducted one of the most fascinating research studies on consciousness. The following text is by a neurosurgeon and professor of neurological surgery and pediatrics, Michael Egnor, MD, at Stony Brook University, describing Libet's experiments:[109]

Libet asked: What happens in the brain when we think? How are electrical signals in the brain related to our thoughts? He was particularly interested in the timing of brain waves and thoughts. Did a brain wave happen at the same moment as the thought, or before, or after?

It was a difficult question to answer. It wasn't hard to measure electrical changes in the brain: that could be done routinely by electrodes on the scalp, and Libet enlisted neurosurgeons to allow him to record signals deep in the brain while patients were awake. The challenge Libet faced was to accurately measure the time interval between the signals and the thoughts. But the signals last only a few milliseconds, and how can you time a thought with that kind of accuracy?

Libet began by choosing a very simple thought: the decision to press a button. He modified an oscilloscope so that a dot circled the screen once each second, and when the subject decided to push the button, he or she noted the location of the dot at the time of the decision. Libet measured the timing of the decision and the timing of the brain waves of many volunteers with accuracy to the tens of milliseconds. Consistently, he found that the conscious decision to push the button was preceded by about half a second by a brain wave, which he called the readiness potential. Then a half-second later the subject became aware of his decision. It appeared at first that the subjects weren't free; their brains made the decision to move, and they followed it.

But Libet looked deeper. He asked his subjects to veto their decision immediately after they made it – to not push the button. Again, the readiness potential appeared a half-second before conscious awareness of the decision to push the button, but Libet found that the veto – he called it "free won't" – had no brain wave corresponding to it.[110]

The brain, then, has activity that corresponds to a pre-conscious urge to do something. But we are free to veto or accept this urge. The motives are material. The veto, and implicitly the acceptance, is an immaterial act of the will.

In summary, Penfield couldn't evoke with all of his electrode pokes an intellect or will in the brain.

Sperry carefully studied patients who'd had their brains split in half and their minds weren't split; Libet, a researcher, couldn't find *free-won't* brain wave activity.

Now, I don't present these studies as proof positive that the part of the mind devoted to the intellect and will isn't in the brain. I present them to show there is scientific evidence to support this theory. There are many scientists who will vigorously dispute the dualist's position. These debates over dualism become so emotional partly because, historically, going back to the Age of Reason during the 18th century, the intelligentsia made a decisive break with religious institutions and beliefs to embrace science. Science relied solely upon the observable and the measurable and nothing else. It became a safe haven. Whenever you cross the line and start talking about nonphysical things, you rustle up the old fears and misconceptions, understandably so. Look at when Freud proclaimed that the belief in God was a psychological need, and that was it: from then on, people who believed in God were perceived as psychologically weak. I hope you get what I mean. When you throw in peoples' religious beliefs, then you add more fuel to the fire. Regardless, I work hard to present deep spiritual matters with two feet on the ground in science and one head in the clouds.

The Radio Analogy

If it's true that the physical brain isn't producing the intellect and will, then these mental functions and probably our wisdom also come from some other "place," wherever that might be – maybe centered somewhere "close by." The Higher Self is in this other "place" and effortlessly works with and maybe controls the brain.

A good analogy between the mind and the brain is the relationship between a radio station and a radio. When you listen to music on the radio, is the source of the music coming from the radio itself? No, the music is coming from the radio station. The station is sending out radio signals (which are electromagnetic waves) that travel through the atmosphere to your radio (today's radio is our smartphone). Your radio uses an antenna and electronic components to pick up these signals. When you turn the radio dial, the radio frequency you tune into determines which stations you receive because each station transmits its unique frequencies. When the radio tunes into a station's frequency, the radio converts the frequencies into sound by using the radio's speakers. The same thing may be true of the intellect and will.

It's my belief that the ego-mind and the Higher Self aren't centered within the brain; instead, they use the brain like a converter or a radio (a radio is a converter). Thus, the brain isn't the source of our insights but just a converter of spiritual energy, coming from a "place" that isn't material to our brain.

The major purpose of the HMJ is to bring to life the dormant neural network that is the powerful receiver for our Higher Self by doing some rewiring and stimulation. When fully stimulated and brought to life, this neural network will easily resonate with our Higher Self and allow it to be experienced daily.

It's comforting to know that our Higher Self is with us all the time, and it's only our brains and hearts that aren't attuned to being able to receive their signals readily. Right now, we are tuned into our false self. But as we rewire our brains to tune to the Higher Self frequency through meditation, then we will start vibrating more and more with our true selves. Now, this will most likely not occur all at once. But over time, it will dominate our consciousness.

My Out-of-Body Experience

I mentioned earlier in the book about an out-of-body experience while I was living in Dodgeville, Wisconsin, practicing optometry. I was sitting in my dentist's chair in a neighboring town, called Mineral Point, when my dentist put a gas mask on me to prepare for a drilling. While I was about to go off to "sleep," he and his assistant left me alone in the room.

Before you know it, I'm floating up on the ceiling, staring down at my body in the chair and then looking over towards Dodgeville, where my family lived. I'm wondering what they are going to do once I'm gone. Luckily, when the dentist came back into the room, I returned immediately to my body. I know what it's like to be thinking and conscious while not in my head and definitely not in my body.

I know this is all a bit "mind-blowing," but so much of who we are and how our consciousness works stretches beyond what our cognitive minds can comprehend. None of this is easy, and it's all open to question.

Can You Ask for Answers?

Is there a preferred way to relate to our Higher Self and ask questions of it? The answer is that it's best to request from the heart, which is one of the best connections and portals to the Higher Self. Also, it's best to be in an alpha state when you do that and ask for a specific answer. Stay present and be patient. Gandhi had to wait seven weeks for an answer regarding the salt tax. Your responses will come. This is really like prayer.

> **Meditation:**
> I invite you to now take three gentle breaths. Open your heart to experience insights! Give yourself the freedom to be wise and to tap knowledge from deep within. Take another three gentle breaths.

Wisdom's Intention

Our intuitive wisdom helps drive us toward answers to our questions. Each of the five spiritual characteristics of our Higher Self supports the others. Love, compassion, joy, inner peace, and intuitive wisdom all work together in tandem and service. It's not only we who are served but also our family, close friends, fellow employees, and our community, both locally and globally.

As people of wisdom, our primary concern is to create a better world, a heart-based world. I firmly believe that each of us has a significant part to play in this process. Our Higher Self knows what part each of us is to play. I strongly urge you, in your meditation, to explore your intentions and how they pertain to this global effort. One of the great silver linings of the COVID pandemic is seeing its worldwide impact and its effect on the planet. We now know how this one "bat out of hell" from Wuhan, China, can disrupt the whole world. This situation is bringing everyone on this planet closer together.

Being universally connected, makes it clear that a global movement to bring about a better world is within our grasp. Solving the pandemic requires a global effort (similarly, global warming requires a collective response). In the newly expanded agenda of worldwide priorities, a heart-based community dedicated to world peace is doable as well. By tapping into our infinite resources of wisdom and doing our inner work, we gain a portal to a new world. Our collective wisdom will tell us what the game plan will be in a whisper. The relevant thing is, will we listen, and respond appropriately?

The Wisdom of Our Bodies

I have referred a few times to how miraculous our bodies are, and it's our consciousness that is the organizing force that maintains the function of our bodies. When we think about the amount of wisdom we have at our disposal, just imagine the wisdom required to make our bodies function in such incredible ways.

As I was writing, I became a bit overwhelmed by all of this. The amount of wisdom we need to solve some of our personal problems is miniscule compared to the challenges the body faces every moment. I mentioned that the body has thirty-seven trillion cells, and one hundred trillion bacteria cells or microbiome (mainly in our gut) we must keep happy and well-behaved. Try to imagine managing that project. In partnership with our spirit, we have to eat correctly, do our physical exercises, and meditate.

Wisdom from the Higher Self

If gaining wisdom was easy, we would all be wise. We are learning key tools for generating wisdom. Our practice can feel like it felt when we first learned to ride a bicycle. When you first started riding a bicycle, you would fall over, and you would say, "How the heck can I do this? This is impossible!" Then you would look around and see that other people were able to do it and realize that *this is possible*. You kept working on it, scraping your elbows and knees, until it suddenly came together. Boom! Just keep the meditation going because practice makes perfect!

Capturing Dreams is Like Capturing Wisdom

My experience with a dream group illustrates how the Higher Self transmits knowledge to us. I joined a dream group about forty years ago, while I was living in Madison, Wisconsin. This group met once a month and had done so for a few years. I joined an established group as a newcomer. The group was composed of five others and were experts in this field, in a sense.

Dreams sometimes refer to areas of your life about which you aren't so aware as they mainly reside in your unconscious mind, and it helps to have other people around who can interpret patterns in your dreams that don't make sense to you. I believe they don't make much sense to you because you have put them out of your mind. After all, you don't want to deal with them. They need an outlet, and your dream world is where they are played out. The group advised me to tell myself to remember my dreams right before I went to sleep and record them right away upon awakening. This reminder helped me to program myself to become conscious of my dreams while they were occurring.

We all have between four to six dreams a night, altogether lasting two hours. It's helpful to have a dream journal right by your bed, just as we keep a journal for our insights in meditation. For several weeks, I was at first unsuccessful in remembering my dreams. Slowly, I started to remember a dream or two, and finally, one incredible morning, I woke up and remembered six full dreams! I was able to write them all down before forgetting them. That was a big accomplishment. And this will be the same way it will happen to you with your increased ability to capture your wisdom as it comes to you.

I believe that our insights are coming to us all day long, but we need to carefully direct our awareness to perceive them. Our Higher Self is constantly trying to figure things out by generating conclusions, solutions, and action plans, and it's up to us to learn how to listen and practice listening. Over time, we will better connect with our inner wisdom, which can only occur when you are fully present – this is what attunement is all about.

The Wisdom of Being Here Now

In the early 1960's, Richard Alpert, a highly respected clinical psychology professor at Harvard, later renamed Ram Dass, and his fellow professor, Timothy Leary, became highly dissatisfied with the level of understanding Western scholars had developed around human consciousness. After discovering the unusual powers psychedelics have on assisting in personal transformation, they collaborated for the next five years conducting extensive research on this subject. Alpert finally realized that after each drug-based trip, he would always come down from it. For him, the transformations were time limited. [111] That is when he decided to travel around India looking for a wise man to help give him more insights. Soon after arriving in India, he was introduced to an American, Bhagavan Dass,[112] who had been living there for some years, studying with several spiritual teachers.

Richard Alpert was impressed with Bhagavan's state of mind and decided to travel with him to meet some of his teachers. While they were driving through the countryside, Alpert said, "Did I ever tell you about the time that I …" and the American cut him off and said, "Just be here, now." Alpert went quiet. Later on, Alpert asked, "When are we going to get to where we are going?" The American said again, "Be here, now!" Alpert said he was getting anxious about how long the trip was taking. The response he received back was, "Emotions come and go!" This conversation is somewhat out of the ordinary, but there is truth and wisdom in that exchange.[113]

As it turned out, Bhagavan introduced Alpert in 1967 to his eventual guru, Neem Karoli Baba, who gave him his new name, Ram Dass, meaning "Servant of God." After spending a lot of time in India studying with his guru, Ram Dass released his famous iconic book, *Be Here Now*, in 1971.

Ram Dass entitled his book, *Be Here Now,* because being in the present moment is essential to sustain a connection with your Higher Self and to be receptive to your intuitive wisdom. While learning the basics in this book and practicing the HMJ program, you may receive an insight and not think it's an insight. Be ready for that. Insights might come in the form of a regular thought. Accept it and open your mind to this learning process. It's like using a muscle that you have never used or have not for a long time. Listen carefully and with focus. Your Higher Self doesn't yell at you – instead, it whispers. That is also the way God communicates with you – in whispers!

Rest in Awareness

I love the phrase, "Rest in awareness." It captures what we are doing when we are fully present. We allow ourselves to rest or be comfortable with who we are, which is awareness at our core. Wisdom isn't available to us when we reside in the past or the future because wisdom comes from the Higher Self. The door to our Higher Self only opens in the present moment. If we get lost in the past or the future, the door to our inner wisdom abruptly slams shut, and we are cut off from a significant source of guidance to living our lives to the fullest. Thus, resting in awareness makes us fully present to who we are, and the flow of wisdom coming through to us from our Higher Self and God.

> **Meditation:**
> I invite you take those three delicious gentle breaths. Now concentrate only on your awareness. Without trying to do anything just rest in your awareness. Take another five breaths as you just be.

Our Inner Resources

Einstein understood how to shift from the ego-mind to the Higher Mind. Although acknowledged as the greatest scientific mind in modern times, he would switch out of his cognitive channel when faced with unresolvable problems. As I noted before, Einstein would pick up his trusty violin to play compositions of Mozart. Einstein and classical music lovers everywhere, over the past couple of centuries, have adored Mozart, probably because the sound vibrations of this spiritual genius gave people access to their Higher Self. This story also highlights the two values chanting and music have: one to help access the Higher Self and the other to quiet the cognitive mind through calming vibrational influences.

Wisdom Flows

Let me repeat a phrase from Gandhi's peace prayer: "My wisdom flows from the highest source." If you access your Higher Self, no matter how old you are, an incredible amount of wisdom is instantly available to you. There is a collective experience that the Higher Self draws upon for resources and nourishment. During the production of the HMJ, I would place myself under a great deal of daily pressure. My ego-mind kept telling me, "You can't do this. You will run out of good ideas. You will have to stop after you run out of fuel." When I opened myself to that endless resource of wisdom available to our Higher Self, I became greatly relieved. Our resources are unlimited. I realized this firsthand while practicing my Wisdom on Demand meditations. I would start my day by letting my Higher Self feed me insights; one right after another they came flowing into me during my meditation. I would then discipline myself to write them down in the morning. Later in the day I would write up a new talk for the next session.

After I had practiced my meditation and kept opening up my wooden box of gold coins inside that I discovered endless resources of wisdom. Now, I have whatever insights I need from my wisdom practice. What a great relief. It gave me the confidence to move forward. This same wisdom resource is available to you, whatever your field of endeavor and personal aspiration. And you know we have a lot of work to do together!

During my depression at nineteen, I was completely unaware of the inner resources I had available to me. My awakening became possible because I was so fed up with my life and so much in pain. I was willing to take a leap and try a whole new reality, leaving everything else behind. Once I incorporated this new reality grounded in truth, I was directed onto a whole new life path. During the next five months, I drew upon Higher Wisdom that just flowed through me. I made progress in activist causes and spiritual growth. Now, all of this happened because I was fortunate enough to discover the wooden box filled with golden coins, which I was sitting on. You are sitting on your treasure as well.

Conclusion

With the Wisdom On Demand meditations, we have completed an overview of our Higher Self's key components. Our objective is to become skilled in experiencing our Higher Self during our waking hours. We will then rest within our awareness and our Higher Self throughout most of the day. Our ego-mind can then shift from being the master to being our servant.

The five spiritual characteristics of the Higher Self are love, compassion, joy, inner peace, plus intuitive wisdom. We will learn to experience and integrate all of these five elements simultaneously to consistently rest in awareness while our Higher Self is being experienced. The ability to do this is similar to how we write music. We choose the best set of notes, and to create chords. Using these chords, we make spiritual music to soothe our souls.

Our journey is about identifying and experiencing each of these spiritual characteristics that make up who we are. We go over them again and again until we master them to find our true selves. In designing future series, these five spiritual characteristics will be woven together into a fabric, creating a tapestry of experiences. This tapestry will finally give us the ability to move from an ego-dominated to a heart-based consciousness. We will eventually learn to experience our Higher Self fully and be real. After we polish our mirror and look into it, we will see a perfectly clear reflection of who we are.

Dr. Zach

Meditation:
Let's learn a little skill that is so important in being in the present moment. Just take your gaze away from the book and find an object to focus on and at the same time take five gentle breaths. And then relax.

13

Emotional Intelligence - Part Two

Anyone can become angry - that is easy. But to be angry with the right person, to the right degree, at the right time, for the right purpose, and in the right way - this isn't easy.

Aristotle

As a refresher, EQ is the ability to understand our conditioned responses, observe our emotions while being in touch with our feelings, and handle interpersonal relationships judiciously and empathetically. In the previous EQ series (Chapter 5), we added the following tools to the equation: the expanded STOP method: **S**top what you are doing, **T**ake a breath, and **O**bserve your thoughts, sensations, or moods by scanning your upper body and locating the areas of greatest sensation and then breathe through that area until the sensation is reduced or fades away. And then **P**roceed with the day.

Rewiring With a Hammer and Chisel

In this series, we add to our EQ toolbox a rewiring process: the ***fully*** *expanded* STOP *method*. While in the meditation state, we first recreate in our mind's eye a particular troubling emotional moment and observe our inner body's responses to it. Then we concentrate on the negatively charged internal representation associated with this emotional moment. We then go mentally to those unwanted internal representations and rewire them. The meditation process of rewiring involves a more hands-on graphic visual process. We do a bit of sculpting/electrical work by knocking out with a hammer our negative internal representations. We then chisel in a new, positive internal representation. We go from being an electrician to a carpenter in order to add a little more graphic imagery to help with the transmutation.

*Every moment I shape my destiny with
a chisel. I'm a carpenter of my own soul.*

Rumi

This process of specific rewiring increases our ability to reprogram our minds to pull out the negative internal representations. These negative images end up being like bad apples in our emotional barrel. The associated negative conditioned responses create situations, relationships, and circumstances that don't work for us. Even though we may want to change them, we are spun back into the same predicaments, over and over again.

And the reason for this conditioned straitjacket is simple. When we experience a traumatic event, a strong neural pathway is laid down in our brains that interprets any similar event in the future in terms of the old one. The prior trauma colors it as being threatening or highly negative. Then we respond, as we have in the past to that event or stimulus, in a defensive and sometimes inappropriate way.

These inappropriate responses are the ones to focus upon because we want our lives to work for us, not against us. It becomes critical to be able to change our emotional patterns of behavior. When we do these exercises, we don't want to activate our avoidance responses. We don't let fear dictate which situations to dodge, because those will probably be the most significant ones.

Every stimulus and response pattern has an internal representation that links the two. These internal representations determine how the stimulus is perceived, whether negatively or positively. If it's negative, the sympathetic nervous system is activated for flight or fight. If it's a positive internal representation, the parasympathetic nervous system will be activated generating a sense of calm and well-being. In the following Frankl quote below he is referring to the internal representations.

Between stimulus and response there is a space. In that space is our power to choose our response. In our response lies our growth and our freedom.
Viktor E. Frankl, Holocaust survivor

Meditation:
Again, sense your inner body. Take three gentle breaths. And now mentally scan your upper body to make an emotional/physical assessment. Now, gently breathe through the area of greatest sensation until that sensation is lessened or disappears.

Increasing our emotional intelligence is exactly what we are doing in this series. The beauty of this part of the practice is we discover the incredible healing powers of our consciousness when directed in the right place and in an appropriate state of awareness. This healing consciousness helps us learn to do the right thing when we are overcome with negative emotions.

First, we have the skill to do this practice because we have learned how to focus our awareness like a laser beam to create desired neural pathways, which was impossible before doing the HMJ. These newly established pathways will positively impact our levels of success and happiness. We will become more contented and more engaged in our personal lives and our workplace. We all want to be happier. My definition of happiness links happiness to the amount of time one spends experiencing one's Higher Self. Maybe that is the definition of being super-happy. Another way to become happier while we are in the ego-mind is transforming our most highly negative inappropriate responses to the world around us into positive ones.

Even after this series is over, we can reprogram ourselves on our own with the new tools we have learned. Each time that we become aware of a conditioned response that keeps hurting us, we can become that sculptor/electrical engineer by knocking out one negative internal representation and carving in a new, positive one. I must say that this process can only be done in a alpha state because it needs for you to be laser focused. The tools we are learning now are endless in their potential value and can transform our responses from the smallest nuisances to our most significant relationships.

Dealing with Anger

When you deal with anger, you need to detach from the idea *you* are angry. Instead of considering that this anger is an integral part of you, consider that you have an emotion that is anger. In the following meditation you will observe this emotion in the same way you did with watching your thoughts going by. This exercise becomes relatively easy as we strengthen our ability to be an observer of our emotions and thoughts instead of being identified with them and being run by them.

> **Meditation:**
> Again, sense your body right now. Now take those three delicious, gentle breaths. Think of something you are angry about. Wait a moment. Now mentally scan your upper body to find where that negative thought created a sensation. If you find it, gently breathe through that sensation until it's lessened or disappears.

Transmuting Anger Into Love

Our anger is a form of energy. Usually, when we experience anger, we aren't lucid. Our spiritual practices will allow us to transform the energy of anger into that of love and/or compassion over time. In being present and mindful, we become focused enough to make that happen. We can apply our powerful transformational process to either our personal lives, or coworkers and work situations. Your transformational ability comes from shining your light of awareness onto those situations you want to make better.

Remember the biggest changes start with your inner work, which you process through awareness. Solutions will begin to take root. Some things will happen immediately, and others will take longer.

In *Emotional Intelligence: Why It Can Matter More than IQ*, Daniel Goleman shows that one's perspective on one's emotional situation, from an observer's standpoint, is a critical step along the path of becoming fully aware.[114]

> *A belligerent samurai, an old Japanese tale goes, once challenged a Zen master to explain the concept of heaven and hell. The monk replied with scorn, "You're nothing but a lout – I can't waste my time with the likes of you!"*

> *His very honor attacked, the samurai flew into a rage and, pulling his sword from its scabbard, yelled, "I could kill you for your impertinence."*

"That," the monk calmly replied, "is hell."

Startled at seeing the truth in what the master pointed out about the fury that had him in its grip, the samurai calmed down, sheathed his sword, and bowed, thanking the monk for the insight.
"And that," said the monk, "is heaven."

The sudden awakening of the samurai to his agitated state illustrates the crucial difference between being caught up in a feeling and becoming aware that you are being swept away by it. Socrates's injunction "Know thyself" speaks to the keystone of emotional intelligence: awareness of one's own feelings as they occur.

The lesson of this story is true to life. Yet, it's difficult to change your behavior patterns once you find yourself swept up in an emotionally conditioned response. This is true for almost everyone. That is why the *fully expanded STOP method* is crucial in changing your most emotionally charged behavior patterns. You rewire yourself while in a peaceful state. In that state, you aren't in the so-called "heat of battle." When future battles do occur, the rewired switch mechanism transforms a negative to a positive response. We can then be fully prepared to deal with the emotional crises that pertain to specific situations prior to their arrival.

> **Meditation:**
> Now take three gentle breaths. Imagine for a moment a major anger that you may hold in your being. Now separate that anger from yourself and hold it out in front of you and breathe into it for a few times and let it evaporate.

As an example, I changed my internal representation of my older brother, Gene. Starting from infancy and continuing while growing up, he would periodically try to make my life miserable. Recently, he admitted he had no empathy for me. I would add that he had no mercy for me. Nevertheless, we reestablished our relationship on a positive footing after a long hiatus. I then applied the *fully expanded STOP method* tool to lock in a love-based relationship. We have been close ever since.

In doing the exercise, I created an image of my brother as a small boy, sitting on my mother's lap in our living room. They both sat in our overstuffed, brown, leather easy chair that we had in our second-floor Bronx apartment. Both my mother and brother held their arms wide open. They were welcoming me to sit on their laps while offering me all their love. This image worked perfectly! When I think about my brother, the first image that comes to mind is the revised scene of my imagination. He has his arms wide open to embrace me with love.

The power of creating new images was illustrated by the story about my new faucet, which made me unhappy. I was disappointed that my friend's faucet would start spraying when he turned it on, and mine didn't. This problem made me sad, but I created in my mind's eye the image that the first normal water flow was an expression of love. Now the softer and normal flow had a caressing sensation, and this positive image allowed me to become happy with my new faucet. Not only that, but it had the unique feature that it seemed to express human qualities of love, affection, and even gentleness, that my friend's faucet didn't have!

Our newly enhanced emotional intelligence is so powerful that it can be regarded as a kind of super-awareness or super-emotional intelligence. It possesses the ability to affect the emotions of others as well positively. An emotionally intelligent person can influence the behaviors of other people as a result. As it pertains to leadership, emotional intelligence has five main elements: self-awareness, self-regulation, motivation, empathy, and social skills.[115]

What we are learning in this series is more than emotional intelligence. By the analogy of being a sculptor/electrical engineer, we are designing new neuronal pathways that create positive results. It's our engineering consciousness that makes this possible through our ability to focus our awareness, as wide as the universe – or in this example, as narrowly as a single neural network. One of the most relevant things to know about our conscious awareness is we will always choose what is right for us when we shine our light on things and come from our Higher Self. If this is true, we can derive great comfort in trusting the great wisdom our Higher Self provides us. I always go back to the miracle of the physical body; how intricate it is, and how all of the moving parts work together in complex synchrony. That same intelligent life force links to our consciousness.

As you go about your day presented with a transformed situation or relationship you've created through your new internal representations, become mindful and acutely aware of the new inner dynamics and new externally changed events you have established. Breathe life into this new internal representation, make it prominent, and give it good energy.

From a HMJ exit suggestion

I hope that these exercises on rewiring negative situations were of interest. We intervened to target the emotional triggers and successfully defused them. It can take time to be successful at this kind of inner work. It won't always be a success immediately, but change will happen with practice.

As the famous adage states;

You give a poor man a fish and you feed him for a

day. You teach him to
fish and you give him an occupation that will
feed him for a lifetime.

Anne Isabella Thackeray Ritchie

Breath Awareness:

Meditation:
Let's do a nice breath awareness exercise. I invite you to count to ten while counting the first inhalation as #1 and the following exhalation as #2 and so on until you get to #10. If you get lost in thought, just return back to the number you remember you were on and continue again to #10.

Mechanics and Benefits

We always have to return to the breath because it's our most effective tool to return to the present moment while playing a big part in maintaining our emotional equilibrium. Breath awareness is like a flue to a chimney that allows hot air and carbon particles from a fireplace to escape to the outside. If you haven't bent down to look up into the chimney from the perspective of the fireplace while trying to avoid soot on your hands and clothes, you probably are unaware of what a flue looks like.

A flue is a metal plate with a hinge, which allows the plate to flap. The flue can open and close the air passageway that connects the fireplace to the chimney.

The flue also has a handle that allows one to adjust its angle, regulating the amount of air to feed the fire while the hot air escapes up the chimney to the outside. When the flue is adjusted just right, the fire burns efficiently; if there isn't enough oxygen flowing, the fire can sputter and go out.

The same thing is true with our bodies. How we breathe, consciously or unconsciously, determines how much oxygen gets into our bodies. The amount of oxygen that gets to our brains has a lot to do with affecting our level of consciousness. When the brain receives just the right amount of oxygen, our ego-minds, designed to protect us from danger, become relaxed; things must be okay if we are getting ample amounts of oxygen. Thus, when we do conscious breathing, our ego-mind begins to go quiet. Most of the time, we want the ego-mind to be quiet so we can consciously connect with our Higher Self; conscious breathing can instantly make that happen.

However, when we become stressed, and fear takes us over, we either take shallow breaths or hold our breaths unconsciously. When our bodies lack oxygen, the amygdala becomes alarmed because something must be wrong and alerts the sympathetic nervous system. Since we are usually caught up in our heads thinking about the future or the past, there is "no one home" in the present moment to have any awareness that your existing distress is due to a failure to breathe properly. When you become mindful in the present moment, you discover that you are "strangling" yourself. Once you gently return your breath back to normal, your stress will decline, and you can return to a sense of well-being.

Breathing is the *one* physical function that is both *involuntary*, which means it goes on by itself, and *voluntary*, which means that we can control our respiration consciously. The breath is *the key* to our conscious control over the autonomic nervous system, the part of our system that lies outside of our awareness and runs entirely unconsciously. The autonomic nervous system has two major components, which include the sympathetic nervous system or "the fight or flight" centers, and the parasympathetic, which is the "rest and digest" or "feed and breed" system. Both are key determinants to our emotional responses and balance.

To positively impact your emotions, you need to harness the breath as the key tool and foundation for your emotional intelligence.

The breath can stimulate the parasympathetic system and quiet the sympathetic system. The breath can help remove stresses in our bodies. The breath can help quiet the ego-mind to keep it out of the way of experiencing our Higher Self. The breath can help us blow away the negative energies in our bodies. The breath can increase the energy we put into certain images and processes that enhance our well-being. Finally, we use our breath to stay in a state of awareness. The breath is like a magic wand!

Forgiveness and Love

There is no love without forgiveness,
and there is no forgiveness without love.

Bryant McGill, author and actor

To experience true love, one must let go of anger and hatred and forgive. To love others requires that we love ourselves. Remember, we have a love projector inside of us that shines out only as brightly as the inner love we have for ourselves.

A lack of forgiveness can have a long-term impact on our personalities – as this anecdote from my childhood illustrates. As a child, out of revenge, I pulled down my brother's pants in front of our friends at summer camp, soon after he had broken his leg. I intended to embarrass him for all of the terrible things he had done to me. I did so at a time when he was weak and vulnerable. All of my camp friends were shocked. They called me "the monster from 20,000 leagues under the sea," riffing on the movie of the same name. I learned a critical lesson: I needed to develop a nice guy persona to get their friendship back and their forgiveness. This was a major turning point in my life and led to my developing more socially acceptable behaviors. However, unconsciously, I didn't forgive myself at that point. It wasn't until I became an adult that I discovered my self-love was weak and that I had to learn to forgive myself as part of my healing process.

Dr. Zach

Residual Anger and Forgiveness

Once positive behavioral patterns begin to replace negative ones, we experience relief and delight. However, there is still the potential for residual anger or resentments over past injuries in our emotional life. Fostering forgiveness and compassion help reinforce positive internal representations. The ego-mind will hold onto anger as a defense mechanism, but the Higher Self will let it go and come from love and compassion. It doesn't mean you need to ignore the fact that you have suffered. But you don't want to walk around carrying hot coals in your hands while they keep burning into your flesh. Let the coals go for the sake of peace. Peace liberates you from the past without denial. We accept past conflicts and misdeeds but without the lingering stress. If our objective is to be fully present, forgiveness is key to letting go of the past.

> **Meditation:**
> Now take three gentle deep breaths. Now take a moment to send love, compassion and forgiveness to a person towards whom you have a lot of negative emotions. Now take three more gentle breaths.

Trauma is Traumatic

Most of us find ourselves in a straitjacket, comprised of a thick fabric of traumatic events and conditioned responses. Luckily, within this fabric, there are strands of change and transformation. There is fertile ground in the spaces that exist between stimulus and response. At the right time, our internal representations can be changed. We may receive a new flow of insights, motivations, and desires which encourage us to take action.

As an adult, my understanding of my childhood family situation became clearer when my brother admitted that he had no empathy for me. His admission and our joint therapy over the phone allowed us to heal our relationship.

Many of us find ourselves in situations that fail to work for us, but we tolerate them anyway. Tolerance isn't always the best solution while enduring degrading circumstances. Sometimes, while meditating on past trauma, you can't pinpoint the context or history in which negative internal representations were generated. They may be derived from an abusive childhood, a chronic family matter, an isolated trauma at any age, or a longer-term source of stress. It's normal for us to stuff these traumatic experiences into our subconscious, so we don't have to face them because we don't know how to deal with them. Also, we are fearful of them. We feel we will be hurt. Why keep having to experience those horrible feelings over and over again? Unfortunately, holding those feelings inside affects us in unseen ways. Often it can be the cause of illness because of all the inner turmoil that is rumbling through our pain body. That is why we want to start uncovering them. Meditation is one of the best ways to process them, so they don't keep us from being happy and healthy.

Dr. Zach

The Complexity of Projections

Quite often what makes our self-awareness work even more difficult is that our conflicts derive from our projections. We tend to blame other people for issues that really stem from within us. When we aren't happy with others, it usually arises from being angry with ourselves. Then we become angry with others around us, and we start fights with them. Maybe not so much about what they are doing, but just because we are irritated with ourselves. It's hard to admit this fact and even sense that our internal issues may play a significant role in creating the external problems.

When we have issues with another, it's a good idea first to ask ourselves whether the problem is with ourselves or the other person, or sometimes both.

Some people do the opposite – they blame themselves for issues that originate with others. If you are someone who is struggling to empathize with another, it will be hard to understand why someone is doing something negative to you and you end up just blaming yourself. A lot of this confusion stems from the striking difference between the way the ego-mind looks at the world compared to the Higher Self. The ego-mind will be in the blame game, blaming either yourself or others. The Higher Self will look at things holistically, from a position of love, and see how the total interaction and environment contributed to the resulting situation.

Through our emotional intelligence exercises, we are directing the energies from inside ourselves in new ways. Again, this process is complicated, but it's best to start with the inner work to see what is going on inside yourself as you begin to sort things out. We should also trust that our Higher Self can work through anything that comes up.

Taking Responsibility:
An Anecdote about Gandhi

Let me share with you this charming story about Gandhi. A mother brought her son to Gandhi, asking Gandhi to urge her son to stop eating so much sugar. Gandhi agreed but told the mother to come back with her son in two weeks. So, they left and returned two weeks later. Then Gandhi obliged her by advising her son to stop eating sugar. The mother thanked Gandhi but, after her son left the room, she asked Gandhi why he had not just told her son to stop eating sugar during the first visit. Gandhi said, "Because I needed the two weeks to stop eating sugar myself." The moral of this story is that Gandhi didn't feel he could give advice which he couldn't follow himself. Gandhi's famous quote puts it this way: "Be the change you want to see in the world."

Psychotherapy

Sometimes there are limitations to meditation and to simply express forgiveness isn't always the answer.

Psychotherapy may be necessary as an adjunct to meditation and spirituality. Some traumas are so severe that we wall them off totally; even if we try hard to search to uncover them, we can't shine the light of awareness upon them. Psychotherapy may be what is best. You can also reach out to your HappCoach to assist you on your journey. If you feel you need outside professionals to help you, we strongly urge you to consult them.

Taking a Stand

There are times when a person needs to stand up and express their outrage to the party who has been the source of the abuse. One must sometimes ask for or demand justice.

> **Meditation:**
> Sense your body right now. Now take three gentle breaths. And now feel how the body feels. Focus on the area in your body with the most pronounced sensation and breath in and out through that area until it feels less intense or disappears.

Conclusion

I feel confident that when meditators finish this series, their emotional intelligence will go up a measurable amount. And that is the best predictor of success at work and general fulfillment in life. I also urge you to return to this series whenever you feel the need to energize a previously worked on internal representation or to work on a new one.

14

Love and Compassion

Embracing Your Higher Self

Grief can be the garden of compassion. If you keep your heart open through everything, your pain can become your greatest ally in your life's search for love and wisdom.[116]

Rumi

This is the first series in which we begin to weave together two of the five essential ingredients of the Higher Self. The meditator weaves love and compassion into a nice pattern so that they can work together. This helps us get to know ourselves better to open the door further to our subconscious and let in more of the sunshine. Let's start off with a quote from the Dalai Lama to emphasize their importance:[117]

Love and compassion are necessities, not luxuries. Without them, humanity can't survive.

This is true because love is the basic vibration of the universe that we surf on and compassion is our ability to overcome the fears of our ego-mind to better express our love and connect with the people around us.

Tell Me More About What Love Is

To experience love is to be truly alive and connected and to actualize our deepest and most innate capacity. Love is the greatest, most powerful force in the universe. There is a paradox. We fear that love will

281

weaken us and make us vulnerable. In many ways, this can be true, but it can also be as Lao Tzu wrote:

Being deeply loved by someone gives you strength, while loving someone deeply gives you courage

.

Lao Tzu

Love helps us go beyond barriers in our daily lives, providing us the ability to cross that line that creates an "us versus them" mentality. Love enables us to come from our hearts to reach out to others; it allows us to go beyond our conditioning to be open to experiencing both the pleasure and the pain of others.

Our practice helps us to love, which is concealed under the veil of fear and illusion. The beauty is that, through meditation, we are returning to our true home, learning to be gentle and inclusive rather than exclusive. It's a practice of truthfulness rather than make-believe. This capacity for love is wisdom that allows us to see things as they are and to return to our true selves.

A Love Relationship

While you are in your ego-mind, a love relationship is like a rollercoaster ride. There is this wild and crazy attraction, repulsion, distraction, and testing back and forth all over again and again. A large part of the challenge is there are three types of love: sexual, possessive, and true love; and they all seem the same at times. Then you are shifting between the ego-mind, wanting control, and the Higher Self, providing relief in the form of just wanting the love to be. If you eventually find a groove, this wild dynamic can begin to calm down and find a balance. But that will probably not last long. Change is a key part of truth. However, being in a state of enlightenment can sure help provide a lot of relief. If your partner becomes enlightened, then that is a whole new ball game!

Tell Me More About Compassion

While we are in love, compassion involves the quivering of the heart toward pain and suffering, our own and another's. What comes with this is a feeling of wholeness and sufficiency. Nurturing our compassion makes us big enough to take in emotional energies without being fragile, shattered or losing all faith. Without compassion, we lose all sense of purpose because we lose connection; we become alone. Compassion is best illuminated when we open our arms and hearts to embrace. Compassion is love in action with a feeling of oneness.

> **Meditation:**
> Sense your body right now. Now, take three gentle breaths. I invite you just for a moment to feel a sense of love and then a sense of compassion. And breathe it into your heart. Do it for three more breaths.

True compassion goes beyond empathy or sympathy. It doesn't happen until sadness merges with joy, the joy of Being beyond form, the joy of eternal life.[118]

Eckhart Tolle

Loving Kindness and Compassion Meditations

The first round of LKM is self-directed. We extend loving-kindness or compassion toward ourselves before we go on to other relationships. We do it this way because we are a radiating light out to others. If our light is dim, we can only send out weak rays of love and compassion. Our LKM and compassion meditations get our hearts going so that we start glowing brightly radiating our love and compassion to others all around us.

Silence Brings Out Our Emotions

Love and compassion fill our bodies with emotion. In our sessions, we provide many stretches of quiet to feel these emotions. We can acknowledge the places where we are stuck. Inevitably, we will twist ourselves into knots when we try to bypass certain feelings and perceptions. The love that would otherwise be available to us becomes withheld. When we set an intention to explore our emotional hot spots, we create a pathway to real love and compassion.

Meditation doesn't eliminate mental and emotional turmoil, but rather provides space, gentleness, and intimacy to experience them. We develop a constructive environment for relating to our emotions and thoughts. Then, we find freedom in how we live our lives instead of letting fear bind us up into these knots. It's a process of accepting your feelings and allowing them to be there. Avoid self-judging by labeling them bad or wrong. Simply name them as painful. Create the space for them, even if they are uncomfortable. Don't take hold of your anger and fixate on it, nor treat it as an enemy to be suppressed. Let difficult feelings simply be there. By being gentle with these feelings, you can face them and allow your awareness to work on them and heal.

Be Aware and Open

It's valuable to permit yourself to be aware of your anger, fear, resentment, or whatever is there. Instead of spiraling down into judgment ("I'm such a terrible person"), you make a gentle observation, something like, "Oh. This is a state of suffering." This acknowledgment opens the door to a compassionate relationship with yourself, which is the foundation for a compassionate relationship with others. We can't use willpower to create the thoughts and feelings that we want to arise. But we can recognize them as they emerge: by turns, frustrating, mixed with fantasy, painful, and changing. By allowing ourselves this simple recognition, we can transform our relationship with ourselves by fostering supportive feelings. This changes everything; we can begin to flow and be open.

Remember that making progress in our emotional life isn't about repressing negative emotions. Progress makes feelings malleable. Instead of feeling hard as steel, they become gauzy, transparent, available for investigation and rewiring. Since there is so little of our true nature in our ego-mind, we need to keep energizing the neural pathways that can receive the spirit energy to experience love, which helps open up our hearts. We allow love and compassion to resonate throughout our being. When we quiet the ego-mind, our Higher Self is opened, we can resonate with newly reinforced images and experiences, and from there, we can make choices on how we want to live our lives.

It Will Come

Sharon Salzberg tells a story about the impact of loving kindness.[119] She had been planning to stay for a full week at the Insight Meditation retreat center that she had just established with some friends in Barre, Massachusetts. During this week, she planned to do the LKM every day for a few hours. Towards the end of the week, she noticed that she was no longer feeling any different. In fact, she was disappointed that the meditation seemed to have no effect on her. Then there was a call to the center. One of their close friends needed help in Boston. So, they all packed up to provide support. In preparing to leave, Sharon hurried upstairs to her bathroom to pack, and when she grabbed a glass jar, it slipped out of her hand and fell on the tile floor, smashing into a hundred pieces. Her inner voice exclaimed, "You are such a klutz, but I love you!" Now that response shocked her because it was an inner response not typical of any she had ever experienced before. At that moment, she realized that her meditation had taken hold.

Getting Our Higher Self and Ego-Mind to Work Together

In our compassion and love exercises, we work on the two sides of ourselves simultaneously, both our Higher Self and our ego-mind. While we teach ourselves to become more centered in our core awareness, we are training our ego-mind to become an assistant in the process so that the two parts of ourselves can work together. This is the key to living out an amazing and purposeful life.

Dr. Barbara Fredrickson's work shows how we can create behavior patterns within each day, which she refers to as *micro-moments of connection.*[120]

> *It's when you share a genuine positive feeling with another living being. Examples are it could be laughing with a friend, or hugging your neighbor with compassion, or it could be smiling at a baby. It doesn't even need to be your baby.*

> *Science suggests that these micro-moments may be more powerful than we think. For example, research finds that when one person's smiles, gestures, and postures*

these behaviors begin to be mirrored by the other person, synchronization is more than skin deep.

When you're connecting with somebody else, your heart rhythms come into sync; your biochemistries go into sync. Even your neural firings go into sync. What's more, that biological resonance of good feeling and goodwill has lasting effects.

This isn't just about your health, because when you're really connecting with someone else, your heart is getting a mini-tune-up, and so is theirs. The more you connect, the more you fortify this wiring to connect, and the more you lower your odds of having a heart attack and increase your odds of living a long, happy, and healthy life. It gives me goosebumps to realize that merely smiling at someone can have significant health consequences.

What fascinates me about what Dr. Fredrickson is referring to, which is all scientifically based, is the fact that when our Higher Self expresses itself through positive human connections, we stimulate the Higher Self in others. Being connected and part of a whole starts to reveal itself. When we charge up human interrelationships, we open our hearts and integrate ourselves with others through compassion. It's a confirmation of our Higher Self and, when we are spreading it around, we all become happier and healthier.

This synchronization of biological functioning that Dr. Fredrickson talks about suggests two things. One is the derivation of the word "conspire," which means "to breathe together." In a similar vein, when my ex-wife, Marlene, was going through her residency in ophthalmology at Mt. Sinai Hospital in New York City, she was so stressed out that she had a terrible time trying to get to sleep. So, when we would get into bed and turn out the lights, I would lie next to her and breathe deeply for an extended period. Eventually, Marlene would start to breathe deeply along with me, which would help put her to sleep. I never told her that at the time because I didn't want her to become conscious of what I was doing. I was conspiring without letting her know.

> **Meditation:**
> As you follow your breath, for a few moments just let go of all of the negativities of day-to-day stress. Bring up an image of who you are at your very best. Consider yourself at your most kind, in your most loving state. Take time now to imagine your ideal self while breathing gently.

Dr. Zach

Compassion Towards a Hated Person

It's essential we reflect on what it means to extend love and compassion toward a person with whom we have a negative relationship, whether at work or in our personal life. This negatively perceived person could be your manager, coworker, family member, or acquaintance. This negative relationship may be generating anger or even hatred. It is the most challenging segment of the loving-kindness and compassion series. How can we hold someone we hate in our hearts?

The Buddha said,

Anger, with its poisoned source and fevered climax, is murderously sweet.[121]

And, of course, his most powerful phrase:

Holding onto anger is like grasping a hot coal with the intent of throwing it at someone else; you are the one who gets burned.[122]

These fascinating and complex images describe an emotion that carries great pain, hurt, and sometimes pleasure. With such complexities, and given such overwhelmingly strong emotions and conditioned responses, how do we overcome these burdens and heal? The most effective way is to turn within because we have an infinite supply of love and compassion to draw upon. Luckily, the light of awareness and forgiveness made up of love is available to us as well. We must remain compassionate toward our emotions and experiences to avoid negatively judging ourselves while going through this process. It's also helpful not to ignore our pain in a rush to forgive. We need to be balanced. One of the most common causes of disease is trying to be too nice to others without getting what you need for yourself. The famous Dr. Bernie Siegel wrote about this over and over again.[123]

Our infinite love and compassion give us strength and guidance. Our practice provides us the tools to support this healing process. The great thing about letting go of our hatreds is that we remove their burden. We feel the lightness of being while strengthening our connections with our beloved community. If we are all one at a deep level, we can reconnect through love with others and experience deep peace. The reality of our deep mutual connections is so much more substantial than the disputes we have with people.

Words Have Meaning

Eskimos have fifty-two words for snow, and the reason is the current condition of the snow can be so critical to their survival. Sanskrit has ninety-six words for love; ancient Persian had eighty; Greek three; and English only one.[124] The fact that English has only one word for love tells me that the ego-mind has been dominating our culture for way too long, weakening our awareness of the subtleties of love. Once our communities become more heart-centered, we will invent new words for love's many facets and subtleties. Maybe a good start is to let the people around us know in what way we love them.

I was recently on a conference call with a group called Happy U, led by Lionel Ketchian, when a gentleman told the story about how he committed to telling his wife a new reason why he loved her every day for one whole year. There were days that he thought he couldn't do it, but he pulled it off. He said it did wonders for their relationship. Could you imagine if we all did that? How much would that change our world? This man's yearlong love interchange with his wife reminded me of the high school teacher's exercise with her students. Magic happens when you become overloaded with love.

> **Meditation:**
> Take a few gentle breaths. Now think about three things you love about yourself. Take another few gentle breaths. Now think about someone you love very much. Think three reasons you love them so much. Now take another few gentle breaths.

The Love Movement of the 1960s

This discussion takes me back to the Spring of 1967 during my Open Arts' days leading up to the famous Summer of Love later that year. I was trying to transform the anti-Vietnam War movement, hoping to convince the movement's leaders to use the power of love in their communications and delivery. The expectation was the movement would be more effective, and we would help end the war quicker. We referred to our efforts as a love movement for just the same reasons discussed above. There was a painfully severe love deficit in our society; emotional love was hardly expressed anywhere. This point was highlighted by a famous photo of a young hippie walking right up to a fully armed US soldier who was assigned to protect the Pentagon Building in DC during a Vietnam War demonstration. The hippie placed the stem of a flower into the soldier's rifle barrel. The incident prompted the phrase "Flower Power," and the new battle cry was "Make love, not war!"

The hippie movement strongly influenced this period, and as you probably guessed already, I was a hippie - a responsible one. I'm proud of the major issues that were raised back then, which are popular now, such as: the love and care of the planet (ecology), vegetarianism (the care of the body through proper nutrition), inner peace and meditation, and the value of Eastern wisdom traditions. Even the use of psychedelics is now starting to show great promise in treating depression and addictions. Their efficacy is now being tested in formal, FDA-approved clinical trials. The substance psilocybin, in micro-doses, is showing positive therapeutic effects.[125]

Overall, the period of the 1960s had strong spiritual messages, and one was a growing awareness that each of us has a Higher Self, a higher consciousness. The spiritual pursuits to discover the Higher Self were split between psychedelic experiences supported by popular music, and the growing widespread interest in meditation.

The pursuit and experimentation for spiritual knowledge and well-designed meditation practices spurred on during that era are being felt right now. Our culture is rapidly embracing meditation and the unique value of our inner work to make our personal and work lives better.

The Importance of Present Awareness with Love and Compassion

Compassion is the part of love that is active; it's the arms and legs of love, which means that our bodies are the vehicles through which love can express itself. Without our bodies, love would just be. To fully take advantage of our bodies, we have learned the importance of being aware of the present moment. It's only through the present moment that we can connect with the emotions that flow through the body as it reacts to our thoughts. If we don't feel these emotions as they occur, we become blind to these positive micro-moments and will fail to build upon them, especially when trying to be compassionate.

The following is an example of how being blind to micro-moments affects our lives. Here, Joe is trying to interact with Fred compassionately:

- Joe is being compassionate to Fred in some way.
- Fred, for some reason, reacts negatively to Joe's compassionate gesture.
- This brings up some past traumatic event in Joe's life.
- Joe has a negative internal representation about it.
- Joe generates a negative thought.
- Joe's body reacts to this negative thought (generates an emotion).
- Since Joe isn't fully present, which he probably isn't, Joe can't feel the emotions in his body because he isn't in the present moment.
- Joe responds back to Fred without knowing how he really feels because he isn't fully present, his responses are totally coming from his defensive, fear-based ego-mind.
- Fred responds to Joe from the same level of disorientation to his own emotions and lack of feelings.
- The interaction keeps up without Joe or Fred knowing what is really going on.

This sad, ridiculous cycle goes on and on. It's how we are living our lives! Concentrating on being present requires practice because the ego-mind, unable to function here, wants to keep pulling us out of the here and now; it must move back and forth between the past and the future. If you want to stay present, it requires steady vigilance to keep the ego-mind from taking control. That is why breath awareness is such a valuable tool. The STOP method, if appropriately implemented, would change the interchange between Joe and Fred completely.

Ruminating as a Way of Life

We know that negative, fear-based thought processes follow a repetitive pattern. The more we think about or ruminate on a negative feeling, like regretting something in the past, the more entrenched the idea becomes. These negative and traumatic thoughts tend to loop; they play themselves out endlessly. As a result, their neural pathways become stronger and more difficult to turn off. Therefore, ideas that cause depression, anxiety, panic, obsessions, and compulsions can become so hard to combat. Along the way, these thoughts stir up emotional as well as physiological reactions.

In the face of looping negative thoughts, we need to cultivate the Higher Self with our practice. If we do our loving-kindness meditation and compassion practice enough, it builds up our positive neural pathways, making them incredibly strong. They become the predominant mindset and short circuit the urge to fall back into a negative state of mind. Of course, all of the myriad tools and skills you have learned by now will be operational to help maintain a calming of the mind.

> **Meditation:**
> Let's again do our three gentle breaths and imagine loving yourself to bits. Now concentrate on the region of your heart and imagine your heart is breathing in and out for another five breaths.

Practice Makes Music

The following musical analogy is a good way to understand how learning to embrace or "play" the Higher Self will unfold as one takes the journey to enlightenment. When we sit down at the piano and play a simple Mozart piece for the first time, it can be frustrating. With more practice, we are soon able to play it better. We really can't feel the music in its entirety because we are just learning the basic movements of the fingers, the beat, and the rhythm. However, after a certain amount of practice, the song begins to take shape. We can finally feel the music and experience what the composer intended to convey, which evokes joy and satisfaction in a job well done.

How Amazing Love and Compassion Can Be

As we get close to the end of this chapter, I wanted you to read this story because it shows how incredible a person can be and the depths of our ability to be loving and compassionate.[126]

Dr. Zach

The Nurse and the Marine

A nurse hurriedly took a young marine to the bedside of an old man and said to him, "Your son is here." The patient was heavily sedated. After a while, with difficulty, the old man opened his eyes. The young marine was standing near his bed and the old man reached out to hold his hand. Seeing this, the young man took his hand and held it. He wrapped his hand around the old man's trembling hand with care and affection. The nurse brought a chair for the marine to sit on beside the old man's bed. Throughout the whole night, the marine sat by the old man's side, holding his hand and comforting him.

Occasionally, the nurse would come to check in on the old man's condition and would suggest to the marine to take a break and get some rest, but he refused. The nurse was touched by the love and affection of the son for his old man.

Later that night, when she came in, she heard that the young man was saying a few gentle words to the old man. The dying old man said nothing, but only held tightly to his hand. Toward dawn, the old man died. The marine released the lifeless hand of the old man and went to the nurse to inform her about the old man's death.

After completing all the formalities, she returned to the young marine and started to offer her sympathies, but the young marine interrupted her and said, "Why are you saying this to me?"

The nurse was startled by his response and hesitated, and then said, "He was your father!"
The marine replied, "No, I don't know him. I never even met him before in my life."

The nurse was confused and asked, "If you don't know him, then why didn't you say something when I took you to him?"

The marine replied, "I knew there had been a mistake, but you were in so much of a rush and, when I saw the old man, I felt that he needed his son, who wasn't there. When he took my hand, I realized that he was too sick to tell whether I was his son or not. Knowing how much he needed his son right near the end of his life, I stayed there.

When someone else needs you... Just be there.

There seems a strong connection between this story and the one about the mother and her son's murderer. In both stories, there is a deep connection between two people that is hard to understand on one level, but on another, it makes all the sense in the world. These people connected on a very deep level through love and compassion. It's a spiritual experience, and on that level a sense of oneness begins to shine through, and it all starts to make sense.

15

Discover Your
Magnificence

Dr. Zach

*Although I still hear voices, I now
accept them as part of myself. And just as I've
come to terms with them – the experiences
they represent and the messages they were
trying to communicate – they have
transformed in character. Today they are
guides and allies, not tormentors.*[127]

Eleanor Langdon, psychologist

In this series, we acknowledge our magnificence in the face of the negative tone of our inner voices. It's the objective of this series to transform our inner voices to become supportive in a loving way. Let's face it, we are incredible beings on many levels, and we deserve to be treated with respect. Throughout our journey, I periodically mention unbelievable facts about our bodies to wake us up to how amazing we are from top to bottom, inside and out. It's incredible when we imagine our consciousness is running our bodies and that we are one: mind, body, soul and God.

It's in our best interests to have our harsh inner critics become supportive guides and allies so that they don't depress us and make us feel terrible. It will also help if they can tone down their activity so that our Higher Self can be heard. We deserve it. It's good to know that the voices we hear are echoes from our parents. They constantly tried to keep us safe and do the right thing, from infancy to adulthood and beyond. Our brains aren't fully formed until we reach the age of twenty-six, so our parents had their hands full for a long time. So, we need to thank them for their love and enduring support.

Awakening and Evolving

There are two major threads that are being woven together on our journey: the awakening and the evolving processes. The awakening process means learning to disidentify or break our identity with our ego-minds or false selves and discover how to identify and experience life through our Higher Self. The evolving process means learning how to live happily, with a great sense of well-being, when we find ourselves during each day stuck in our ego-minds. So, we are developing a dual strategy to deal with each state of mind.

The Inner Critic

Previously, I gave you a definition of happiness, which is determined by the amount of time one spends each day with the Higher Self, as compared to the time spent with one's ego-mind. A key skill to improve our level of happiness in this evolving process involves dealing with our inner critics or judges.

In this series of meditations, we learn how to deal with our inner critics. It's helpful in this process to honor the ego-mind because it teaches us things and gets us to behave in a way that keeps us alive and well. For our survival, when we were fighting off saber-toothed tigers on the plains in Africa, we had to be negatively biased, on full alert, to stay alive. But as our civilizations have evolved, our average day doesn't require a constant and intensive oversight or battering by our inner critics. We all know what that is like. Our critics constantly pester us with, "Do this," and "Don't do that!" The critics ask what is wrong with you and suspect that you may be an idiot for such and such reason. And the usual, "Why you don't exercise more?" and "Why are you eating so much sugar? You know better!"

This constant bombardment of one critical thought after another plays a big role in determining how happy we are and how much peace we have in our lives. Inevitably, we feel bad about ourselves. A lot of people hate themselves because of it! You can easily see why we have a tough time discovering our magnificence during this repetitive mind assault of critical thoughts.

In our practice, our inner critics introduce themselves. Actually, we have a team of critics trying to oversee our lives, but we make the realistic assumption that they don't know how to do it lovingly and compassionately. During this series, we become skilled in teaching the inner critics a way to offer their advice in a loving and supportive way to lessen their negative impact on us and improve their effectiveness.[128] We also learn to discern the valuable from the destructive comments. Of course, the most powerful tool we can use is to shine our light of awareness on the activity of our inner critics. The best way to help heal our tortured ego-minds and bring a sense of order into play.

The Underground Chatter

As a result of these exercises, I realized my critical chatter occurs below my level of awareness. My critics were going underground, and that is why sometimes they are impossible to deal with. When our critics go underground, they can cause our overall malaise or depression to deepen because we don't know from where they are coming.

When we stuff our fears and self-criticisms out of sight and out of mind, or when we try to run away from them, they can have adverse effects. In our sessions, we flush the critics out into the open and confront them. We are looking to work with them without trying to shut them up. If we try to shut them up, we will only send them back underground again, giving them more power. This is essential to understand this in dealing with fear in general. Don't let fear push them away as a shortcut but use your light of awareness to bring them out to have a healthy conversation. Don't ever forget that the self-organizing power of our consciousness is designed to do what works best for us. There is nothing more powerful than our consciousness. By the way, don't forget, we are consciousness; be with your power!

Dr. Zach

Facing it Head-On

When I focused on a few critical comments, which were negatively impacting my life, I became quite emotional; a lot of fear came up for me about failing and my body began to shake. I had to stand still and take it in. I scanned my body. I breathed positive energy through the areas of most pain until this emotional moment passed. I do know and feel that the process has given me a lot of relief. My fear of failure has receded, and I'm still alive! Facing the fear didn't kill me.

The moment you accept what troubles you've been given, the door will open.

Rumi

This quote says it all in so many ways. I know it's hard to face up to and experience the voices of our inner critics. But, as we now know well, the light of awareness is infinitely more powerful than fear. Fear exists when we are unconscious of who we are. When we come into the present moment, the shadows where fear hides out disappear into the light. That is exactly what we are doing in this practice. We are shining the light of our awareness onto our team of inner critics, who possess all the inner fears, judgments, and criticisms that bring us down and sap our energies. Our ego-mind is rooted in the fears, judgments, and criticisms with that we identify. These negative things aren't who we are. We are so much more. This practice allows us to uncover the negative illusions about ourselves and face them. Yes, there will be some or a lot of uncomfortable feelings, and fears will surface. But you will overcome and get through them because you are magnificent! We have been discovering our magnificence throughout this journey. We must step into that fire and keep moving through it and not let our fears stop us.

Meditation:
Take a gentle breath and then, more deeply, another one. Breathing brings relaxation throughout your body. Now think about a criticism your inner critic is always telling you and say back to the inner critic that you get it and it would be nice if the critic could say it in a more loving way. Now take three more gentle breaths.

Developing a Supportive Relationship with Our Critics

Concerning our inner critics, we are learning to become acute observers, to see exactly how the critics behave. In a sophisticated way, we work with the critics to help them become more positive in their approach. The more reasonable they become, the less separation will exist between our inner and outer environment. Conversely, negative, fear-based thoughts have the opposite effect. They create more separation, which is the false reality that the ego-mind wants us to believe is true. Remember, the ego-mind is trying to create an illusion to separate us from the world around us and to be defensive to people and situations.

By watching the inner critics, we become more conscious. When we are unconscious, the ego-mind dominates. Our practice will focus more and more on our state of presence to better know when we are in our ego-mind and when we are in our Higher Self. We must transfer the success of our inner work into our daily lives. This dialogue with our inner critics is a crucial steppingstone in helping us move along on our journey.

16

Mindfulness in the Workplace

*If you just sit and observe, you will see
how restless your mind is. If you try to calm
it, it only makes it worse, but over time it does
calm and, when it does, there's room to hear
more subtle things – that's when your
intuition starts to blossom, and you start to
see things more clearly and be in the present
more. Your mind just slows down, and you
see a tremendous expanse in the moment. You
see so much more than you could see before.
It's a discipline; you have to practice it.*[129]

Steve Jobs

> **Meditation:**
> For our last meditation, let's show Steve that we can
> quiet our mind with a nice counting of our breath
> exercise. Let's count to ten with #1 being our first
> inbreath and #2 is our first outbreath and so on. If
> you get lost in thought, just return to the number you
> last remember you were on and then continue to #10.
> How do you feel? Great job!

Creativity and Its Value in the Business World

To emphasize the importance of meditation in nurturing creativity and wisdom, in 2010 IBM did a global CEO survey, requesting *the* most crucial factor for their company's future success. Fifteen hundred CEOs from sixty different countries and thirty-three different industries placed *creativity* above rigor, management discipline, integrity, or even vision –

"successfully navigating an increasingly complex world will require creativity."[130] The need for creativity and wisdom isn't only for the executive team but also for every employee.

It's helpful to know that creativity can't function when stress levels are too high. To protect employees and reduce their stress levels, it is necessary to foster resilience and collaboration. The only way to approach this effectively is to view it holistically. Each of these components can't be dealt with selectively. The corporate environment is an ecosystem and needs to be approached as an integrated system. The best way to effectively deal with fostering creativity is through meditation.

Meditation will foster:
- Creativity
- Collaboration
- Resilience
- Compassion
- Love
- Focus
- Engagement
- Equanimity
- physical health
- emotional intelligence

Dr. Zach

The Value of Emotional Intelligence in the Workplace

Since Dan Goleman's NY Times bestselling book on emotional intelligence (EQ), the business world has awakened to the value of EQ as potentially superior to IQ. Moreover, studies show that EQ can be more relevant to success than cognitive IQ; EQ maybe twice as significant in creating stellar performance as pure intellect or even expertise.[131] The value that increased EQ contributes to the improvement in the workplace experience can't be overstated.

In a 2011 CareerBuilder survey of more than 2,600 hiring managers and human resource professionals, 71% stated that they valued EQ in an employee over IQ, and 59% claimed they would pass up a candidate with a high IQ but low EQ.[132]

Because of the significant value of increasing the EQ of any workforce, the HBJ, the business version, includes two series devoted to increasing an employee's EQ. These two series provide guided visualizations to allow employees to work through any primary emotional issues they may have with their manager, team, and company as a whole. It's an opportunity to do inner work to cultivate more constructive relationships by nurturing positive emotions, better communication, and improved collaboration. In response, managers who participate in the HBJ may start feeling better about their teams, and teams will be feeling better about their managers.

Businesses Adopt Meditation as a Benefit

Corporate meditation programs are becoming quite widespread throughout the US. The best indicator on the subject is the 2017 survey by Fidelity Investments and the National Business Group on Health, which predicted that 44% of large corporations would be offering meditation as an employee benefit by the end of that year. If that trend continued, over fifty percent of the largest companies would be offering meditation to their employees. I'm amazed by that prediction. It's an encouraging sign that employers are interested in meditation to care for their employees' mental well-being and as a resource for improving their work environment.

Our Changing Culture

Based upon the CDC survey, in the US there are currently over thirty million people practicing yoga, and thirty million are meditating.[133] Rapidly, these practices are becoming an integral part of the US culture.

Mark Bertolini's Fascinating Story[134]

To fully capture the potential of the mindfulness in business revolution, it's appropriate to tell the story of the ex-CEO and Chairman of Aetna Insurance, Mark Bertolini. In 2004, Mark was involved in a brutal skiing accident. He skied right off the slopes into a tree, before plunging sixty feet into a ravine. He landed on his back in a pool of icy water, where he went unconscious. It took two hours for the rescue crew to find him and get him to the hospital. They thought he would become a quadriplegic.

After being in a coma for a week, his doctors told him that he was lucky that he had fallen into the pool of water. The cooling of his battered spine kept the inflammatory process to a minimum, where ordinarily, his spinal cord would have torn itself apart due to swelling. So, even though he broke his neck in five spots, miraculously, he walked out of the hospital within two weeks under his own power. However, as Mark so delicately put it, the accident "ripped my nerve roots out of my spinal cord to my right arm." The ripped nerves hurt his right arm so much that it left him with this "incredible" neuropathic pain. "It felt like a blow torch was focused on my whole right arm all day long!"

Mark was discharged and sent home with pain medications – seven types, including fentanyl, vicodin, and oxycodone – which he had been prescribed to take daily. Unfortunately, the pills did next to nothing for his pain except to make him more aware of it. From Mark's perspective, his condition had destroyed his quality of life. His physicians tried every pain management approach possible, to no avail. Then, one day a friend suggested he try yoga and meditation. He decided why not. Nothing else was working, and he had nothing to lose. Finally, after only a few weeks, it worked! He could still feel the pain, but now he was able to isolate it and start enjoying life again.

As fate would have it, three years later, he became president and CEO of Aetna, which had 50,000 employees at the time. After Mark became CEO, he told his chief medical officer (CMO) that he wanted everyone to do meditation and yoga. His CMO pushed back and told him, "Mark, you can't dictate to every employee that they have to do this, although we can do it on a volunteer basis."

Over the next twenty-four months, 12,500 employees, or 25% of the company, were doing meditation and yoga regularly. The effect on the whole company was profound. People were reporting amazingly positive things happening in their personal lives and in the whole corporate culture. Overwhelmed by their program's impact, Mark contacted a research group at Duke University to study its effects.[135] After Duke concluded their study, the results showed that there was a $3,000 benefit from increased productivity for each employee, and $2,000 from reduced medical claims from their high-risk group of employees – making a total of $5,000 of benefits per year from their high-risk group. To get an overall reading on stress, they measured everyone's associated cortisol levels. This indicated employee stress levels had markedly been reduced.

Aetna's stock rose 500% from when the company started their yoga and meditation program until the company was sold to CVS in 2018 for $70 billion.

One of the key takeaways from this story is that a meditation program can be most successful if the president or CEO buys into the program and sets the example for the rest of the company. Then its full impact can be felt. Mark wrote:

> *The greatest rewards have been in what we actually accomplished: defying norms to create a better workplace, designing a new approach for engagement with the community, and reimagining our mission to build a healthier world.*[136]

HBJ & HMJ – Business and Personal Self-Development Version

The HBJ, the business version, guides employees to bring up specific people-related issues to work on. They get the opportunity in their minds' eye to focus on their manager, buddies, team, and the whole company. This is done during the Loving Kindness, the Compassion, and the two Emotional Intelligence series.

The HBJ allocates a meaningful amount of time for the employee/manager relationship because this interaction is the most fragile and, potentially, the most disruptive.[137] More employees quit their jobs over their negative relationship with their manager than any other factor.

Value of Having a Personal Self-Development Version

Quite often, employees doing the HBJ program ask if their family members could download the app. If their family members don't work in a corporate environment, it's a cool option for them to have the opportunity to use the personal self-development version. In addition, it's a positive reinforcement for employees to have family members doing the HMJ as well. It becomes a family affair.

After an employee finishes the corporate version, I have found they start the personal self-development one. The two versions together amount to one hundred and fifty hours of guided meditations.

In Summary

Meditation increases our EQ and helps us produce higher levels of creativity, stellar performance, enlightened leadership, and happiness in the workplace. I refer to this as rising to a "genius levels of performance." Such benefits can be gained simply through employees maintaining a steady practice.

HappCo's Business Program

HappCo offers a full-service program for businesses to launch and maintain a meditation program. The program includes:

- Initial presentation to establish program and teaching
- Launch and enrollment resources
- Full reporting on each department and division
- Weekly evening Zoom calls to answer questions
- Assessment surveys
- Coaches track and support each employee
- Dedicated coaches for each company

Glossary

Altered state – Changing your behavior for a limited period of time and then it fades away.

Altered trait – An existing human characteristic that is true to your nature that was not being expressed but finally comes alive, is expressed, and persists. When we embrace our Higher Self and express it for most of the day (enlightenment), that is the best example of an altered trait.

Breath awareness – Concentrating on the breathing process. You can feel your breath by focusing on the air coming in and out of your nose, the rising and falling of your chest, or the expansion and contraction of your belly.

Compassion & Empathy - Empathy is a skill and capacity to understand or feel what another person is experiencing from within the other person's frame of reference. Empathy involves walking in another's shoes to feel the suffering or joy of another without necessarily doing anything to help or to support that person. There is no action component to empathy. When you feel compassion, you are also in the other person's shoes and feel the suffering of another, and you have a desire to take action to relieve another's suffering.

Ego-mind - For our work and discussions, the ego-mind is this self- consciousness system that is functioning in a state of illusion. It is living in the past and future, not in the present moment, and is based on fear as opposed to our Higher Self, which is based on love. The ego-mind considers itself your Higher Self, but it is not. The ego-mind is not even aware that a true Higher Self exists. It neither understands nor cares about this confusion. It is programmed to dominate your consciousness and stay dominant.

Emotional Intelligence - The ability to monitor one's feelings and effectively manage one's emotions while recognizing the emotions of others. It also gives us the ability to discriminate among our emotions and guide our thinking and actions.

Enlightenment – The ability to embrace your Higher Self for most of the day and be able to quiet the ego-mind, and have it become a servant rather than dominate your consciousness by fooling you into thinking it is who you are.

Higher Consciousness – is another way to describe your Higher Self.

Higher Self – Our true consciousness which is based upon love, compassion, joy, inner peace, and intuitive wisdom.

Illusory sense of self – Through evolution our consciousness has evolved such that our ego-mind dominates our sense of self. The ego-mind is a false sense of self. It is based upon fear and cannot maintain its awareness in the present moment, so it mainly focuses upon the past and future. Our goal is to embrace our Higher Self, live in the present moment, dispel this illusion, and live life in a state of love.

Inner body – It is an energy field that you can feel when you are fully mindful of the present moment and focus your attention on the sensations, feelings, and moods you experience when you place your attention on your entire body. It is the best place to concentrate on to know how you are doing.

Meditation – The practice of meditation, referred to in this book, is the technique of quieting the ego-mind and allowing us to experience our Higher Self. Our ego-minds dominate our normal waking state and produce an electrical brain wave pattern that oscillates at a rate of 15-40 cycles per second called beta waves. In meditation, when we are experiencing our Higher Selves, our brain waves slow down to 9-14 cycles per second, referred to as alpha waves. When we go into a deeper state of meditation, we generate waves of between 5-8 per second called theta waves. It is in these slower states we can do our inner work, which is spiritual in nature.

In meditation, we begin to follow the breath to allow the mind to focus inwardly while still awake and alert. We are not concentrating on the external world or the events taking place around us. Meditation requires our inner state to be still and highly focused helping the cognitive mind to become silent and our Higher Self to be fully present.

Mindfulness – Being fully in the present moment aware of thoughts, sensations, and feelings in our bodies.

Mindfulness & Meditation - Mindfulness and meditation do overlap in many ways. When we do a body/scan meditation, we are being in a mindful state as we become aware of the thoughts, sensations, and feelings in our bodies. We also use mindfulness to help us enter a deep state of meditation as we begin each session. In fact, during the day it is very important to allow ourselves to dwell in our "inner body", which requires us to be mindful. Going back to the inner body is a great way to continue being mindful during the day. So, mindfulness could be considered a subset of meditation. In our goal of becoming enlightened, being in a mindful state for most of the day is what we are learning to achieve.

Portal – is any pathway, or tool, or skill you use to embrace your Higher Self. Breath awareness is the best portal to your Higher Self.

Resilience – The ability to maintain a sense of equilibrium and inner peace while being impacted with negative emotions, feelings, and events around you.

Spirit - If consciousness is who we are, then the feelings we have when we experience spirit should be how we define spirit. Spirit is our life energy comprised of love, compassion, joy, inner peace, and intuitive wisdom - all in one package.

Spiritual journey – The experiences you have while figuring out that you are a spiritual being living in a physical body. The journey entails discovering your true self and finally being able to embrace your Higher Self.

Epilogue

The next step in your journey is to decide what to do with all of this new information, insights, and resources. This book is valuable as a comprehensive primer and companion resource for the HMJ. When you go ahead and download the HMJ app, which I strongly urge you to do, this book will greatly enhance your meditation experience. When you start doing the HMJ, I would use this book as a resource to help answer any questions you might have along the way. This book's in-depth descriptions will help you better appreciate the value of your experiences and how it fits into the overall process of attaining enlightenment. This book and the HMJ, are dual resources and will assist you in transforming your life and your company.

The Time is Now

Like now, the 1960s was another great moment of opportunity to transform this world. We planted the seeds we desperately need for survival by creating today's understanding, mindsets, and strategies. Those seeds took root, grew up, and now we are ready to harvest them: the caring for the planet through robust ecological programs; a firm commitment to renewable energy; the cultivation of love and compassion for all people through promoting meaningful meditation programs in the schools and workplaces; promoting good foods and proper nutritional support and education; promoting world peace and disarmament; and last but not least the time to establish racial equality – it's about time. The most important question is, are we going to step up now to meet these enormous challenges?

I must go back to Einstein's quote, "We cannot solve our problems with the same thinking [consciousness] we used when we created them." It's also true that one of the definitions of insanity is doing the same thing repeatedly and expecting different results. So, it's our essential responsibility to transform our consciousness to save our species. Remember Dr. Fredrickson's, Christakos', and Fowler's work, where they emphasized how powerful we can be to positively influence each other in ways that can be earthshaking. If we work together to change our communities and companies to bring out the Higher Self, we have that capacity to nurture the spirit in everyone around us.

If you subscribe to this belief, the wonderful thing is that the steps to take on our path to survival are pretty straightforward and relatively easy. Reading this book wasn't hard. Spending twenty minutes per day meditating isn't like pulling teeth. Our job is clear. Start the HappCo Meditation Journey program, recommend other people to read this book, and follow up by urging them to start meditating. Just remember, if we are going to solve all the messes we have created - from environmental issues, to pandemics, to racial disharmony, to military wars and threats to nuclear conflicts - we need to change our state of consciousness. If we don't, we are destined to repeat these outcomes repeatedly. According to the scientists, we don't have much choice but to get active to get these jobs done.

Raising Consciousness

Our ego-minds created a world of conflict and strife while the human population is lost in this state of illusion. We have the tools now to shine our light of awareness on this disabling blind spot and begin to clearly see our way out of this mess. The pathway to solving most of the major problems and conflicts we face today is rooted in our ability to tame our ego-mind and bring out in full force our Higher Self! This is our clarion call!

Establishing a Clear Intention

Each one of us needs to make a clear intention to take responsibility for our individual consciousness and support the people around us to do the same. It's clear that we need to raise our collective consciousness to be able to think more creatively, act more lovingly, live more compassionately, and be more peaceful as we take on the challenges ahead. Remember that intentions are the vessel in which we hold these ideas and desires and to help make them become realized. There is power in this step, and we should take it seriously. In the HMJ, one of the first things you will do before you begin your meditation is to write down your intention in doing your practice.

Becoming a consciousness advocate is a great thing to become. Now that this book is completed, I'm going to dive into the social media world and get the word out that this package is available to everyone.

Recommended Practice Protocol

If you are serious about becoming enlightened, I recommend doing one session (each session runs about twenty-two minutes) in the morning and repeat the same session in the evening, right before going to bed. You will experience a significant change in your life doing it only once per day, but if you want to increase the probability of attaining enlightenment significantly, I would follow the twice-per-day regimen. When you increase the time, you are meditating, you are doing a finer tune-up to your receivers, improving the connection to your Higher Self.

Reminder

So, after reading this book, if you do resonate with what I have written about, I support you in downloading the HMJ app to get started! I also have a Facebook page where you can share your insights and experiences. You can follow me on Twitter and Instagram, too.

Thanks for going on this book journey with me. I hope you have enjoyed it. Also, I hope to get to know you and provide you with follow-up support on your spiritual journey. If you want me to provide additional support to you or your company, please contact me at: drzach@happco.com. If you want to download the HMJ app, go to the App Store or Google Play and search for HappCo Meditation Journey.

In conclusion

I mentioned that I have been experimenting all my life to find the right way to help people become happier and to find peace. And it's now clear that it's the inner work that is key to find our Higher Self to bring out the love within. From there, we can project outward what's inside each one of us to transform the world. We can do it!

Finishing up this book brings me a bit of sorrow for some reason. I guess it's because I realize the amount of work and effort that has gone into this project. I only hope and pray people get the full value that this book and, more significantly, what the HMJ program provides. I firmly believe there is a potential breakthrough available to us that can change the course of history. This awakening process is the essential building block we need to create the new world we all dream about and can feel and taste.

"All you need is love, love
Love is all you need"[138]

Thank you and God bless you and stay well!

Acknowledgments

Dr. Zach

I have been influenced by a lot of great people possessing wonderfully creative minds. My spiritual path hasn't taken me to an Eastern monastery or ashram because I was awakened with the help of a good friend, John Zwicky, whose compassion offered me his great wisdom that helped save me from a deep, suicidal depression. I owe him a tremendous amount of gratitude. Ever since my awakening, I have been listening to my inner voices, drawing upon the resources of our collective wisdom, been to many retreats and talks, read a lot of books, and have done a lot of meditating.

I dedicated this book to my mother not only because she was a great person but because her activism and commitment to the well-being of all people was the model by which I have lived my activist life. I helped organize many projects and organizations directed towards helping people in their struggles and our planet's well-being.

My mother operated within the classical mode of social and political activism. She used marches, demonstrations, supporting and electing politicians to make the changes she felt needed to be made. She was a progressive, and so am I.

But there was a major difference between the two of us because of my spiritual awakening that changed the course of my life. My mother was an atheist and so was my father, Irving; consequently, I was brought up as one. The interesting thing is that my activism was quite similar to my mom's course of action for most of my life, but mine had a touch more spirituality thrown in.

Our activist paths began to diverge when I realized that peoples' inner work is primary, and the other activities are critical. Still, they must be placed on a secondary level of priorities while implementing the other activities simultaneously. Each activity feeds upon the others. They are all synergistic.

My brother, Gene, defined me as a spiritual artist. I think that is a good way to describe me. Gene, a serious spiritual traveler, was very supportive and diligent in helping me edit and put this book together. We had many hours of stimulating discussions, which helped me make this book coherent and consistent.

One of the greatest influences on helping me make sense out of my awakening has been Eckhart Tolle. Whenever I picked up his "Power of Now" and "The New Earth" to read, I resonated with each and every idea and concept. One of the great things about his writing is that he has a German engineers' mindset. He breaks down paradoxical and spiritual concepts with precision. The downside is that his writings are too concentrated for me. I needed to read each book twenty times to absorb them fully. I'm not complaining because I don't think I would have been able to create the HMJ without his insights. What is also noteworthy is that Eckhart relied a great deal upon his own spiritual awakenings for guidance and didn't become a monk or have formal spiritual training. His journey has similarities to mine, and it didn't hold him back from becoming one of the great spiritual teachers of our time.

I need to make a special callout to Ram Dass, who is no longer with us in body. His life and the work he did bringing Eastern thought to us was outstanding. He was one of the greatest teachers of spirit we ever had. A real treat is going on YouTube and watching some of the talks he gave before he had a stroke.

In creating the HMJ, I have been gathering the wisdom and approaches that meditation masters, mainly in the West, have developed. Some of them took meditations they learned from their training as monks while they lived in monasteries in the East. We now have a large body of meditations that are a blend of Eastern and Western influences. So, I was able to draw upon this cultural blend as I developed my program inspired by meditations and insights from that good old infinite source of intuitive wisdom that is available to all of us.

Fresh ideas carried me along as the HMJ began to emerge. For example, I learned a nice rhythm to body scanning meditation while taking Jon Kabat Zinn's MBSR program. I modified it to fit into the Mind/Body Integration Series. I learned some relaxation processes from listening to some of Headspace's approaches to introducing meditations. I took the traditional Loving Kindness Meditation Series, which has been around for centuries, and modified that a bit in a way that felt right to me. Then I took a bit from Zinn's STOP method and expanded it to include ways to integrate it into the Emotional Intelligence Series. I took a simple self-awareness process and expanded it to allow us to reprogram ourselves to break free from our conditioned responses. These conditioned responses bind us up into lifelong habits that constrain our growth and ability to live our lives the way we so choose to live them.

Then there is the Compassion Series that I modeled after the Loving Kindness Series. After reading the *Joy on Demand* book by Chade-Meng Tan, it gave me a perfect model to compose a robust Joy On Demand Series, filled with twenty joyous guided meditations. Then the Peace Now Series was an easy one for me since I was known for a long time as a peacemaker. Having organized and run three not-for-profit peace organizations over a forty-year period, teaching inner peace was easy for me. The Wisdom on Demand Series came to me through experimenting with my personal meditations, drawing upon our collective wisdom resources to create this series. In addition, I began to weave the five key spiritual elements into each other by first starting with the Loving Kindness/Compassion Series. The purpose of this weaving is to teach people to start learning how to experience their Higher Self by weaving in the love threads, the compassion threads, the joy threads, the peace threads, and the wisdom threads, all on one loom. When these different threads are woven together, you produce a strong, beautiful, and supportive fabric. You can wrap it around yourself and feel loved and enlightened.

The last series, called Discovering Your Magnificence, was inspired by the great work by Mark Coleman in his book, *Make Peace With Your Mind.* I developed a series based upon creating dialogues with the different voices in your head that drive you nuts and begin to teach these voices to treat you with respect and love, so you learn from them without being driven crazy.

The whole creative process of producing the HMJ was a thrill. I remember, during the two months I spent producing the Loving Kindness Meditation Series, I was living each day repeating and recording twenty sessions in a row. By the time I was finished with the recordings, my heart was so filled with love that I declared that I had the best job in the world.

In some ways, this is a wonderful time to be alive because of all the great groundbreaking research and discoveries that are pushing and questioning the basic foundations of scientific beliefs, while we experience the new, exciting, and exploding interest in spiritual exploration. The books and meditations that I have read and practiced have been so impactful on me. I have provided a bibliography at the end of the book, if you would like to read some great work.

I don't have the space to detail each of these additional great teachers, but here is a list of people who have helped me greatly during my journey through the books they have written. I feel I'm only standing on their shoulders; they have allowed me to see. The following teachers are: Mark Bertolini, Mark Coleman, Werner Erhard, Jon Kabat-Zinn, Jack Kornfield, Sharon Salzberg, Dr. Bernie Siegel, Chade-Meng Tan and Shinzen Young, to name but a few.

I would be remiss if I didn't mention the great research work conducted and books written by Deepak Chopra, Nicholas Christakos, Richard Davidson, Barbara Fredrickson, James Fowler and Dan Goleman.
For Romana Maharshi for teaching simplicity.

God, for the creating, the love, power, and herding us along the way to peace and enlightenment.

Joya Stevensen, my main editor, who was great to work with and who took all of my individual talks and stories and helped me make this into a cohesive book.

For my old best friend, Danny Stein, who met me the next morning after my awakening and reminded me that I told him excitedly, "I figured out everything except death!" He still reminds me to this day that I haven't figured that one out yet.

For another old friend, Jimmy Jerving, who on his own went through the whole book and made constructive edits to help improve the quality of this book.

I can't finish this acknowledgment section without mentioning my wonderful six children -

Dr. Zach

Samara, Louis, Elijah, Juliana, Olivia and Alexander - who are the light of my life. They have had to put up with a lot, but I must say they have been there for me, and I couldn't love them anymore than I do! I must mention my three incredibly wonderful grandchildren Sophia, Eli, and Lyla - bless them all.

Last, but not least, is my ex-wife, Marlene, who I'm dating now. Marlene has been there for me on some of my most meaningful adventures. I appreciate all that she has put up with and that she still loves me and wants to be with me.

Thanks again for taking the time to read this book and taking action! Stay well, be loved, and become enlightened!

Notes

[1] https://www.jneurosci.org/content/35/5/2074.

[2] Merriam-Webster's Update Edition (2020).

[3] https://reformjudaism.org/exodus-not-fiction

[4] John 8:23. Holy Bible. English Standard Version

[5] Chopra, Deepak & Kafatos, Menas. *You Are the Universe: Discovering Your Cosmic Self and Why It Matters* (New York: Harmony, 2017), 71.

[6] Chopra, Deepak, *You Are the Universe*, 98).

[7] Einstein, Albert. *The World As I See It.* (Secaucus, NJ: Carol Publishing Group, 1999). 28-29.

[8] Chopra, *You Are the Universe*, 108.

[9] "Professor Agassiz on the *Origin of Species, American Journal of Sciences,* 2nd ser., XXX (160), 154.

[10] Gould, Stephen Jay. *The Structure of Evolutionary Theory*; Stephen Jay Gould, "Is a New and General Theory of Evolution Emerging?" *Paleobiology* 6, no. 1 (1980): 120.

[11] Meyer, Stephen C., *Darwin's Doubts; the Explosive Origin of Animal Life and the Case for Intelligent Design* (New York, NY: HarperCollins Publishers Ltd., 2013).

[12] Meyer, Stephen C., *SIGNATURE IN THE CELL: DNA and the Evidence for Intelligent Design.* (New York, NY HarperCollins Publishers Ltd., 2009)

[13] Tolle, Eckhart. *The Power of Now: A Guide to Spiritual Enlightenment* (Novato, CA: New World Library 1999), 154

[14] https://www.goodreads.com/quotes/6809246-to-enjoy-good-health-to-bring-true-happiness-to-one-s

[15] Freud, Sigmund. *The Standard Edition of the Complete Psychological Works of Sigmund Freud.* Vol. XIX (1999) James Strachey, Gen. Ed

[16] Malpas, J. & Davidson, Donald. *The Stanford Encyclopedia of Philosophy* (Winter 2012 Edition), Edward N. Zalta (ed.).

[17] Armstrong, Karen. *A History of God* (New York: Ballantine Books 1993), 357.

[18] Wright, Robert. *Why Buddhism is True: The Science and Philosophy of Meditation and Enlightenment* (New York: Simon & Schuster, 2017), 60.

[19] Wright, *Why Buddhism is True,* 63-4.

[20] Pathways to the Spirit series. This 10/23/98 lecture is presented by Dr. Robert A.V. Thurman, a professor of religion at Columbia

[21] "Tolle, Eckhart, A New Earth: Awakening to Your Life's Purpose (New York: Penguin Publishing Group, 2008), 94-95."

[22] Goleman, *Altered Traits*, 240. For an overview of the research, please see: Richard Davidson and A. Lutz, "Buddha's Brain: Neuroplasticity and Meditation," *IEEE signal processing magazine* 25 (2008) 176-174.

[23] Keysers, C. & Gazzola V. "Hebbian learning and predictive mirror neurons for actions, sensations and emotions," *Philos Trans R Soc Lond B Biol Sci.* (April 28, 2014): 369. doi:10.1098/rstb.2013.0175

[24] Yang, C., Barrós-Loscertales, A. & Li, M., *et al.* "Alterations in Brain Structure and Amplitude of Low-frequency after 8 weeks of Mindfulness Meditation Training in Meditation-Naïve Subjects," *Sci Rep* 9 (2019). https://doi.org/10.1038/s41598-019-47470-4

[25] http://www.openculture.com/2019/05/mapping-emotions-in-the-body.html

[26] Kornfield, Jack, *The Wise Heart: A Guide to the Universal Teachings of Buddhist Psychology* (New York: Random House, 2009), 35.

[27] Dass, Ram, *Polishing the Mirror: How to Live from Your Spiritual Heart* (Boulder, CO: Sounds True, 2013), 12.

[28] Kabat-Zinn, Jon. *Wherever You Go, There You Are: Mindfulness Meditation In Everyday Life*. Hachette Books. Kindle Edition:24

[29] http://www.openculture.com/2019/05/mapping-emotions-in-the-body.html

[30] https://www.health.harvard.edu/mind-and-mood/protect-your-brain-from-stress

[31] Chopra, *You Are the Universe,* 71.

[32] Duhigg, Charles. *The Power of Habit: Why We Do What We Do in Life and Business* (New York: Random House Publishing Group, 2014), 21.

[33] Duhigg, *The Power of Habit*, 122.

[34] https://www.health.harvard.edu/blog/mindfulness-meditation-helps-fight-insomnia-improves-sleep-201502187726

[35] https://www.optimize.me/quotes/martin-seligman/21574-habits-of-thinking-need-not-be-forever/

[36] 2020 Merriam Webster Dictionary.

[37] Siegel, Bernie S. *Love, Medicine and Miracles* (New York: William Morrow Paperbacks 1998), 75.

[38] Patel, Jainish & Patel, Prittesh. (2019). Consequences of Repression of Emotion: Physical Health, Mental Health and General Well Being. *International Journal of Psychotherapy Practice and Research* - 1(3):16-21.

[39] Dass, Ram, *Polishing the Mirror,* 9.

[40] CEOs and their top management team: Sigal G. Barsade, Andrew J. Ward, et al. "To Your Heart's Content: A Mode of Affective Diversity in Top Management Teams," *Administrative Science Quarterly* 45 (2000): 802–836.

[41] The analysis linking climate to business performance: David McClelland, "Identifying Competencies with Behavioral-Event Interviews," Psychological Science 9 (1998): 331–339; Daniel Williams, "Leadership for the 21st Century: Life Insurance Leadership Study" (Boston: LOMA/Hay Group, 1995).

[42] The analysis linking climate to business performance: David McClelland, "Identifying Competencies with Behavioral-Event Interviews," *Psychological*

Science 9 (1998): 331–339; Daniel Williams, "Leadership for the 21st Century: Life Insurance Leadership Study" (Boston: LOMA/Hay Group, 1995).

[43] Tolle, *The Power of Now*, 110.

[44] Tolle, *Power of Now*, 36-37.

[45] Tolle, *A New Earth*, 159.

[46] Jung, Carl. *Collected Works* vol. 14 (1970), <u>*Mysterium Coniunctionis*</u> (1956), ¶372, 278.

[47] Divan-i-Kaber Vol 20. Rumi, transl. Nevit Oguz Ergin, (Los Angeles: Echo Publications 2002).

[48] Fredrickson, Barbara. *Love 2.0* (New York: Hudson Street Press, 2013), 23.

[49] Fredrickson, B. L., Cohn, M. A., Coffey, K. A., Pek, J., & Finkel, S. M. (2008). Open hearts build lives: Positive emotions, induced through loving-kindness meditation, build consequential personal resources. *Journal of Personality and Social Psychology,* 95(5), 1045–1062. https://doi.org/10.1037/a0013262.

[50] B. L. Fredrickson, "What good are positive emotions," *Review of General Psychology* 2 (1998): 300-19; B. L. B. L. Fredrickson, "The role of positive emotions in positive psychology: The broaden-and-build theory," *American Psychologist* 56 (2001): 218-26.

[51] Fredrickson, Barbara. *Positivity* (New York: Harmony, 2009), 16.

[52] Fredrickson, "What good are positive emotions," and "The role of positive emotions in positive psychology: The broaden-and-build theory."

[53] Seligman, Martin. *Authentic Happiness* (New York: Free Press, 2002).

[54] Christakis ,Nicholas A. & Fowler, James H. *Connected: The Surprising Power of Our Social Networks and How They Shape Our Lives* (New York: Little, Brown, and Company, 2011), 28.

[55] Christakis, *Connected*, 51.

[56] Christakis, *Connected,* 26-28.

[57] Kornfield, *The Wise Heart*, 15.

[58] www.theparentscircle.org

[59] https://www.thecut.com/2018/03/the-history-of-the-six-degrees-of-separation-study.html
https://hbr.org/2003/02/the-science-behind-six-degrees

[60] Walcott, Derek. *Collected Poems 1948-1984* (New York: Farrar, Straus and Giroux, 1987).

[61] Lama, Dalai & Tutu, Desmond. *The Book of Joy: Lasting Happiness in a Changing World* (New York: Penguin, 2016), 270.

[62] https://www.nature.com/articles/news.2008.684

[63] Wallace, B. Alan. *Tibetan Buddhism from the Ground Up: A Practical Approach for Modern Life* (New York: Wisdom, 2016), 241.

[64] Lowen, Alexander. *The Voice of the Body* (New York: The Alexander Lowen Foundation, 2012), 258.

[65] https://www.sciencedaily.com/releases/1998/02/980227055013.htm

[66] Chopra, *You Are the Universe,*171.

[67] Goleman, *Altered Traits,* 268-269; See also: J. K. Hamlin et al., "Social Evaluation by Preverbal Infants," *Nature* 450 (2007): 557–59; doi:10.1038/nature06288.

[68] Wallace, B. Alan. *Attention Revolution, Unlocking the Power of the Focused Mind* (New York: Wisdom, 2006), XVIII-XVIX.

[69] Wallace, *Attention Revolution,*, XVIII-XVIX.

[70] Goleman, *Altered Traits*, 139.

[71] https://positivepsychology.com/measure-happiness-tests-surveys/

[72] Lyubomirsky, Sonja. *The How of Happiness* (New York: Penguin, 2007), 68.

[73] https://positivepsychology.com/gratitude-research/

[74] Tolle, *Power of Now*, 56-58.

[75] https://www.brainyquote.com/quotes/albert_einstein_122243

[76] https://www.goodreads.com/quotes/2464342-in-louisville-at-the-corner-of-fourth-and-walnut-in

[77] Fallon, James H., *The Psychopath Inside* (New York: Penguin, 2013). There's literature linking a lack of interpersonal empathy to psychopathology. The definition of empathy, in such contexts, is not the same as the definition employed here.

[78] Trzeciak, Stephen & Massarelli, Anthony. *Compassionomics: The Revolutionary Scientific Evidence that Caring Makes a Difference* (Pensacola: Studer Group, 2019), 21.

[79] Trzeciak, Compassionomics, 20.

[80] https://www.wattpad.com/user/EmmanuelAghado

[81] https://www.jcf.org/works/quote/the-key-to-the-grail/

[82] Goleman, *Altered Traits*, 101.

[83] "How do loving kindness and compassion relate to one another?," posted by Jane, *Habits for Wellbeing*, date not

given. https://www.habitsforwellbeing.com/how-do-loving-kindness-and-compassion-relate-to-one-another/

[84] Klimecki, Olga et al. "Differential Pattern of Functional Brain Plasticity after Compassion and Empathy Training," *Social Cognitive and Affective Neuroscience* 9:6 (June 2014): 873–79; doi:10.1093/scan/nst060.

[85] Kelm, Zak, Womer, James, Walter, Jennifer K., & Feudtner, Chris. "Interventions to Cultivate Physician Empathy: A Systematic Review." *BMC Medical Education* 14 (October 14, 2014): 219.

[86] https://buddhaimonia.com/blog/zen-stories-important-life-lessons

[87]

Tolle, *A New Earth*, 230.

[88] Tan, Chade-Meng. *Joy on Demand: The Art of Discovering the Happiness Within* (New York: Harper Collins, 2017), 2.

[89] Fredrickson, Barbara, *Positivity* (New York: Harmony, 2009), 12.

[90] Tan, *Joy on Demand*, 126.

[91] Brickman, P., Coates, D., & Janoff-Bulman, R. "Lottery winners and accident victims: Is happiness relative?" *Journal of Personality and Social Psychology*, *36*.8 (1978): 917–927. https://doi.org/10.1037/0022-3514.36.8.917

[92] Tan, *Joy on Demand*, 109.

[93] https://www.virgin.com/disruptors/dalai-lama-and-importance-compassion-education

[94] Tolle, *Power of Now*, 11.

[95] Conwell, Russell Herman, *Acres of Diamonds: Our Everyday Opportunities*, c.1890, Reprint (Digireads, 2004), 2.

[96] Ito, T., Larsen J., et al. "Negative Information Weighs More Heavily on the Brain. Journal of personality and social psychology," 75 (1998): 887-900. 10.1037/0022-3514.75.4.887.

[97] Kornfield, *Wise Heart*, 11.

[98] https://www.moralstories.org/sometimes-just-let/

[99] Byner, Witter, *The Way of Life* (New York: Tarcher, 1986).

[100] Tan, Chade-Meng. *Search Inside Yourself :The Unexpected Path to Achieving Success, Happiness (and World Peace)* (New York: Harper, 2012), 2.

[101] Tan, *Search Inside Yourself*, 235.

[102] Goleman, *Altered Traits*, 305.

[103] Kwak, S., Lee, TY, & Jung, WH, et al. "The Immediate and Sustained Positive Effects of Meditation on Resilience Are Mediated by Changes in the Resting Brain," *Front Hum Neurosci.* 13 (2019) doi:10.3389/fnhum.2019.00101

[104] https://mariaerving.com/synchronicity-is-always-happening/

[105] Creswell, J., et al., "Alterations in Resting-State Functional Connectivity Link Mindfulness Meditation With Reduced Interleukin-6: A Randomized Controlled Trial," *Biological Psychiatry,* vol. 80. 1,(2002): 53 - 61.

[106] https://www.npr.org/2013/06/14/191614360/decoding-the-most-complex-object-in-the-universe

[107] https://mindmatters.ai/2019/09/was-famous-old-evidence-against-free-will-just-debunked/

[108] https://www.nobelprize.org/prizes/medicine/1981/sperry/facts/

[109] https://mindmatters.ai/2020/02/pioneer-neuroscientists-believed-the-mind-is-more-than-the-brain/

[110] Libet, Benjamin (1985). "Unconscious Cerebral Initiative and the Role of Conscious Will in Voluntary Action". *The Behavioral and Brain Sciences.* **8** (4): 529–566.

[111] Dass, *Polishing the Mirror,* 13.

[112] Dass, *Polishing the Mirror,* 21.

[113] Ram Dass, *Be Here Now* (New York: Harper Collins, 1971), 32.

[114] Goleman, *Emotional Intelligence*, 46.

[115] Goleman, *Emotional Intelligence*, 15.

[116] https://www.brainyquote.com/quotes/rumi_597890

[117] https://www.brainyquote.com/quotes/dalai_lama_121172

[118] Tolle, *Power of Now*, 197.

[119] Salzberg, Sharon, *Real Love* (New York: Flatiron Books, 2017), 22.

[120] Sharon Salzberg quotes a talk by Barbara Fredrickson. See: Salzberg, Sharon. *Real Love*, 108-109.

[121] Salzberg, Sharon, *Lovingkindness* (Boulder, Co: Shambhala, 1995), 86.

[122] https://quoteinvestigator.com/2018/06/18/hot/
The attribution is disputed.

[123] Siegel, Bernie S. *Love, Medicine and Miracles* (New York: William Morrow, 1986), 71.

[124] Johnson, Robert, *The Fisher King and the Handless Maiden* (Harper Collins, 2010), 129.

[125] https://hopkinspsychedelic.org

[126] "English Stories," Sept. 25, 2018, Facebook Post.
https://www.facebook.com/270235497158027/photos/pb.27023549715802
7.-
2207520000.1572844209./272569390257971/?type=3&eid=ARARrJNhwt0lvt
YliMTCELtLk0ZMgLYtdstPpgoJ7cvXy2m0P-
EveRWW3KnJCkNW_T66Z2beJzo3fQaj

[127] https://www.psychologytoday.com/us/blog/rethinking-mental-health/201602/eleanor-longden-recovery-oriented-approaches

[128] Coleman, Mark, *Make Peace with Your Mind* (Novato, CA: New World Library 2016), 148.

[129] Isaacson, Walter & Jobs, Steve. *Steve Jobs* (New York, Simon and Schuster, 2011), 49.

[130] https://www-03.ibm.com/press/us/en/pressrelease/31670.wss

[131] Joseph, Dana & Newman, Daniel, "Emotional Intelligence: An Integrative Meta-Analysis and Cascading Model," *The Journal of Applied Psychology*, 95 (2010): 54-78. 10.1037/a0017286.

[132] Golem, Daniel. *Emotional Intelligence*, See also https://www.careerbuilder.com/share/aboutus/pressreleasesdetail.aspx?id=pr652&sd=8/18/2011&ed=08/18/2011

[133] https://www.cdc.gov/nchs/pressroom/nchs_press_releases/2018/201811_Yoga_Meditation.htm

[134] Bertolini, Mark, *Mission-Driven Leadership* (New York: Currency, 2019), 76.

[135] Wolever, R. Q., Bobinet, K.J., McCabe K., Mackenzie, E. R., Fekete E., Kusnick, C. A., & Baime M., "Effective and viable mind-body stress reduction in the workplace: A randomized controlled trial," *Journal of Occupational Health Psychology, 17.2* (2012): 246–258.

[136] Bertolini, *Mission Driven Leadership*, 6.

[137] https://www.inc.com/marcel-schwantes/why-are-your-employees-quitting-a-study-says-it-comes-down-to-any-of-these-6-reasons.html

[138] John Lennon, 1967, *All You Need Is Love*, Parlaphone, single.

Bibliography

Bertolini, Mark. *Mission-Driven Leadership*. New York: Penguin Random House, 2019.

Christakis, Nicholas A. and James H. Fowler. *Connected: The Surprising Power of Our Social Networks and How They Shape Our Lives.* New York: Little, Brown and Company, 2009.

Chopra, Deepak and Menos Kafatos. *You Are the Universe: Discovering Your Cosmic Self and Why It Matters.* New York: Penguin Random House, 2017.

Coleman, Mark. *Make Peace with Your Mind: How Mindfulness and Compassion Can Free You From Your Inner Critic.* Novator, CA: New World Library, 2016.

Dass, Ram. *Be Here Now*. New York: HarperOne, 1971.

Dass, Ram. *Polishing the Mirror: How to Live from Your Spiritual Heart*. Boulder: Sounds True, 2013.

Fredrickson, Barbara. *Love 2.0: Finding Happiness and Health in Moments of Connection.* London: Penguin Publishing Group, 2013.

Fredrickson, Barbara. *Positivity*. New York: Harmony Publishing, 2009.

Goleman, Daniel and Richard J. Davidson. *Altered Traits: Science Reveals How Meditation Changes Your Mind, Brain, and Body.* New York: Penguin Publishing Group, 2017.

Goleman, Daniel. *Emotional Intelligence*. New York: Random House Publishing Group, 1995.

Harris, Bill. *The New Science of Super Awareness*. Beaverton, OR: Centerpointe Press, 2009.

Kabat-Zinn, Jon. *Wherever You Go, There You Are: Mindfulness Meditation In Everyday Life*. Westport, CT: Hyperion, 1994.

Kornfield, Jack. *The Wise Heart: A Guide to the Universal Teachings of Buddhist Psychology.* New York: Random House Publishing Group, 2008.

Lama, Dalai. *The Book of Joy*. New York: Penguin Publishing Group, 2016.

Maharshi, Ramana. *Be As You Are (Arkana)*. London: Penguin Books Ltd., 1989.

Salzberg, Sharon. *Real Happiness: The Power of Meditation*. New York: Workman Publishing, 2011.

Salzberg, Sharon. *Real Love: The Art of Mindful Connection*. New York: Flatiron Books, 2017.

Siegel, Bernie S. *Love, Medicine and Miracles*. New York: William Morrow Paperbacks, 1966.

Tan, Chade-Meng. *Joy on Demand: The Art of Discovering the Happiness Within.* New York: HarperCollins, 2016.

Tan, Chade-Meng. Search Inside Yourself: *The Unexpected Path to Achieving Success, Happiness (and World Peace)*. New York: HarperCollins, 2012.

Tolle, Eckhart. *A New Earth: Awakening to Your Life's Purpose*. New York: Penguin Publishing Group, 2005.

Tolle, Eckhart. *The Power of Now: A Guide to Spiritual Enlightenment*. Novato, CA: New World Library, 1999.

Trzeciak, Stephen and Anthony Massarelli. *Compassionomics: The Revolutionary Scientific Evidence that Caring Makes a Difference*. Pennsacola, FL: Studer Group, 2019.

Tzu, Lao. *The Way of Life: Translated by Witter Byner*. New York: Capricorn Books, 1944.

Young, Shinzen. *The Science of Enlightenment: How Meditation Works*. Boulder: Sounds True, 2018.